Finally, a book not only for the executive in transition but any executive looking to advance their career that provides a real-world "how-to" on networking, branding (or re-branding) oneself, and making lasting connections with others. This is not just a book but a reference tool that should be kept close by at all times.

Todd Rielly
Former Divisional President, Wachovia

This book is a powerful and practical tool in helping the executive understand who he is, what he is worth, and how to maximize his strengths in the search for the job that fulfills him. The important lesson of the book is recognizing that it is not about your resume or what you did in the past as much as it is about people, you, and your own network.

John Wood
President, The Playfair Group

Whacked Again! *is crammed full of useful information for the job seeker. As a freelance CFO, I am constantly looking for new clients (jobs). I refer to Jim's book frequently for tips on presenting myself physically, verbally, and in writing to help close new business. I highly recommend* Whacked Again!

John Coleman
President and Founder, Fiscal Control

I enjoyed reading your book, and I'm impressed with all the relevant points you make. I will incorporate them in my personal life and professional career. These are valuable business skills necessary for career success and for doing business in the future economy!

Martin Schmidler
VP of Information Technology, UniPro Food Service, Inc.

A reference guide for anyone in transition, Whacked Again! *gives practical advice to help focus one's efforts on proven techniques for improving the odds of landing your next job.*

Wayne Brunson
Controller, Golden Peanut Company

True to his CFO style, Jim presents a concise, no-nonsense dose of reality and a compelling call to action.

Patricia Decker
Principal, Commerce Design Group LLC

Jim lays out a clear process for accurately discovering and presenting who you are, what you do, and how you can help an organization achieve its goals. He walks you through a process of development, marketing, and sales for yourself that follows what successful companies would use to market their products or services. Being out of work for whatever reason can be a confusing and stressful time. Whacked Again! *is a valuable guide providing a structured process for reassessing and repackaging yourself. It makes sense when your situation doesn't.* Whacked Again! *made me slow down and approach moving on using a thorough and thoughtful process. The extra time is well worth it!*

Jim Risler
Director, Skywire Software

Renowned Executive Coach Jim Villwock masterfully leads executives through the fundamentals of self-marketing using a palatable and straightforward approach. This easy-to-use guide is a unique and invaluable tool to anyone employed or looking for employment.

Clark Christensen
Chief Financial Officer, PS Energy Group, Inc.

Whacked Again!

Secrets to Getting Back on the Executive Saddle

Jim Villwock

Whacked Again!
Secrets to Getting Back on the Executive Saddle
by Jim Villwock

Printed in the United States of America

ISBN 978-1-60647-494-5

www.xulonpress.com

To my wife, Martha, who is the love of my life.

Thank you for all your help.

Contents

Acknowledgments

When an author writes his first book, he has many people to thank.

To members of the Financial Executive Networking Group and Kettering, thank you for allowing me to work with you and to learn from you. I have tried to credit everyone for their help. In case you were missed, my apologies.

To Martin Schmidler, Todd Rielly, Jim Lynch, and John Hughes, thank you for your review and suggestions. You have made this book more valuable to everyone.

To each executive draft reader, thank you for your comments and input.

Introduction

The world has changed. The average executive is in the saddle for two to three years or less. Job stability is increasingly an oxymoron.

The pace of these changes appears to be accelerating. The old ways of getting back into a new saddle are working less and less. Those who use old paradigms are often treated as a commodity.

So what are the new paradigms? How can I get the job that excites me? How can I stand out in an increasingly competitive environment? How can I step above the limitations of job boards, recruiters, company applications, and job placement services?

Are there secrets that the most successful executives use? In a word, yes.

You may have heard of several of the concepts we will discuss, but who has sat down with you to walk you through the confusion? Who has shown you a road map that you can understand and follow? For most executives, this may be the first time. *Whacked Again!* is designed to be that roadmap to help you find the best next opportunity.

Most executives I know are "A" players. Given the big picture, roadmap, tools, and behind-the-scene rationale, they can do the rest. This book is written for you, my friends, and their friends.

Fellow executives want the bottom line with explanations as to why actions should be taken and simple tactical steps to reach their goal. I have tried to provide such a format. The material could easily be expanded. Some books cover only a topic or two. This book is designed to provide a strategic umbrella and enough explanation in following chapters to help you apply the principles uniquely to your situation.

Who is the target audience? Any executive, from a small company to a large company, can benefit. The principles apply to everyone. That includes directors, vice presidents, and C-level staff.

Is the material relevant to non-executives? The concepts discussed can apply to a new college graduate, a person leaving the military, or anyone trying to learn how to communicate their value. Obviously, with fewer years of experience, this audience will have more difficulty understanding their passion, value, and achievement stories. However, this road map will provide you the framework to develop your ongoing message as you move up the ladder and compete in the marketplace.

Is the content limited to job seekers? No. Eighty percent of these concepts are also true for employed executives, consultants, relationship sales, and most business-to-business relationships. Another title for the book could be *How to Succeed in Business*. The focus is on transition executives but the applications are universal.

Finally, consider this material to be "insider information." These secrets are the type usually communicated to sons and daughters of those in power – to give them an advantage over others. With this information, you now have the knowledge to help level the playing field. What you do with it is up to you.

If one or more of these secrets helps you, what should you do? I recommend you consider telling all your friends and associates about *Whacked Again!* If you help others become more successful, you may have created friends who will be willing to help you for years to come.

Chapter One

Strategic Overview

Today's Reality

It has been said that today's worker will change careers multiple times during their working life. Even in the same field, workers are often finding that the idea of spending twenty to thirty years at a company is becoming extinct. Unless you are in the military or government services, it is highly likely that you will not be that exception.

I have had the pleasure of working with a high-level financial executive networking group (29,000+ members) and a "C-level" executive networking group (1,200+ members) for years. The comments I am making include my personal observations and those of many whom I have known. The truth is often unpleasant, but reality is what we have to deal with every day. This book is designed to help you succeed in today's difficult times.

For example, one common statement today is that the average life of a CFO in a company is two years. Depending upon the economy, we have seen this as low as eighteen months (1.5 years). We have also heard that the average time to obtain a new job is one month for every $10,000 of salary.

For executives, that means being out of work for a year is not uncommon.

If we do the math, that means working for two years and looking for a job for a year, followed by working for two years and looking for a job for a year. Now multiply the financial impact. If you are making $100,000 a year, then your average real income is only $67,000 – less when you consider paying taxes on higher-income years.

Further, we have seen a tendency of companies to "eliminate positions" for those over fifty years of age, and somehow they never seem to hire anyone over age fifty. I am sure it is not done on purpose. It must just be a coincidence.

For many of our parents, the years from fifty to sixty-five were the high-income earning years. For us, we may find ourselves "unemployable" during the years from age fifty to sixty-five. This may not be because of our value or performance but because our income can be replaced by a lower-paid, younger person.

Today, the simple term is being "whacked." Causes vary widely such as downsizing, right-sizing, "not a team player," resigning due to many factors, occasionally a true personnel issue, or actual performance issues.

The trends today include technology improvements, globalization, mergers, acquisitions, outsourcing, and increased competition. Sometimes the "right-sizing" is done simply to provide signals of proper corporate management for Wall Street or to puff up "profits" to maximize personal executive bonus payouts.

The favorable trend is that baby boomer retirements will create a growing need for workers in the next few years. So the "whacking" of one person may become an opportunity for his replacement.

Yesterday's Experience No Longer Applies

For many professions, prior backgrounds are no longer sufficient for future company needs. For example, knowing the Fortran computer language is considered as relevant as riding a horse and buggy. Some companies may still use such an ancient program, but finding a company looking for a Fortran programmer is like finding the needle in a haystack.

In some cases, not having the latest software language, a foreign language, or Sarbanes-Oxly experience eliminates an otherwise highly qualified candidate simply because their background does not match the checklist used by recruiters or human resources to screen out candidates prior to interviewing.

That means if you do not have the latest skills or experiences, competing against others (who do have those skills and experiences) will be at a minimum frustrating and often a waste of time – even if your other experiences or skills could provide a greater overall value to a company. In other words, you have to get through the gatekeepers to make your case. Most of us do not have the skills to get by those filters.

So we have a problem. Many of us are outstanding performers and hard workers. If our prior job did not provide the new skills and experiences, then we are disadvantaged. Because we worked long hours and were usually loyal to our company, most of us did not develop the social and communication skills that are needed in today's changing world to compete for new jobs.

If we do find a job, it may not be long before we are "whacked again." Learning how to get back into the saddle is the new life skill that is worth its weight in gold—literally.

Opportunities Ahead

If we lack specific experiences, we can retrain or perform contract work to be able to dress up our resume. That may be required and could lead to your next job.

Some who lack skills but are not willing to retrain or perform contract work often settle for a lower-paying job and are happy to have it. After all, the pressure of incoming bills and family needs usually continues to grow.

The real opportunity is to learn how to propel yourself above others, to propel your career, and to enjoy what you are doing. With the turmoil in today's reality, those who learn these skills will find that the opportunities tomorrow can be brighter than they can imagine.

New Skills = Personal Competitive Advantage

Think about the people in companies who seem to be promoted regardless of performance. Outside of marrying the boss's daughter, having a different value system, or being a "yes" man, how did that happen?

Usually it was because the person had more in common with superiors, knew how to communicate in their language, and learned how to market effectively what they did. In other words, they got noticed and communicated their value to higher levels of management.

What we are going to discuss is not how to be dishonest or insincere, or how to climb over each other's backs, but how to work hard, add value, and get rewarded for it.

The key to finding a new job or getting promoted in an existing job (to beat the two-year average) is to *add* to your skill set the same skills and methods used by businesses every day to win the competitive battle against other companies in the marketplace.

We will not make an honest person dishonest. We will help honest people stay honest while being more successful. These skills and methods will help you to find new jobs and rise in the ranks, and they will even help in the home and community.

The bottom line is that these skills and methods will help your personal competitive advantage.

Road Map to Success

The following chart outlines the steps we recommend you consider.

For those who want the easiest path to "getting back on the executive saddle," feel free to skip those areas that sound too hard or time-consuming.

For those who recognize the significance of what I am proposing and wish to be advantaged over the vast majority of job seekers, I strongly suggest that you take each area seriously.

Like any investment (education, financial, or skill development), these steps are not ninety-day wonders. Instead, they are a lifestyle that will be new to most (and therefore hard at first) but very satisfying and enjoyable over time.

Just as important, I believe you will understand their value in not only getting back on a saddle, but getting back onto a saddle on a horse you will enjoy.

Finally, these steps will help you be prepared to change horses as often as required. It is a good feeling to know you can have more control over your future as you continue honing your new skills.

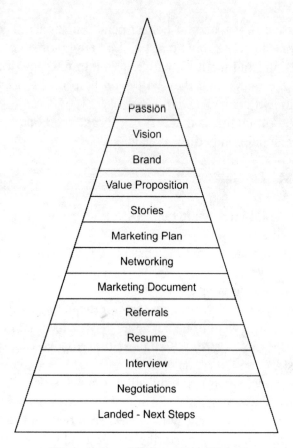

Hierarchy of Transition Steps

The Higher Your Value, The Higher The Required Steps

The rest of this chapter is an overview of the Hierarchy of Transition Steps. Examples and more detailed discussion are included as each step is further discussed by chapter.

Passion

Have you ever shaken hands with someone having a limp (fish) hand? What was your conclusion? Were you impressed? Did they leave a favorable impression?

I personally have the same reaction to someone who talks about what they do without any passion. We hear that 80 percent of Americans hate their job. Why would I want to hire one of those?

If you have no passion about what you are doing, it shows. It shows in your speech and your posture. It shouts, "I just want a job – can you give me one?"

If America turns socialist, that will be what happens. In the meantime, for those who wish to grow a business and make a profit in a highly competitive world, the first real question is whether you are passionate about being a part of a dynamic team. Otherwise you are perceived as dead weight that pulls down others around you rather than putting your shoulder to common goals.

Passionate people enjoy their work, contribute to the success of the team, and are a very rare commodity. If you are passionate about what you do – and know how to show it—you will be far ahead of the rest of the pack.

Vision

Everyone has passions. Many passions are not marketable skills. For example, I may love golf but unless I can play at the professional level I need to find another passion for something that I can demonstrate I have the skills and experience for to add value to an employer.

Once you understand which of your passions are marketable, the next step will be to develop a vision of how to translate that passion into where you want to be. Notice that your vision may be what you have been doing, in the same field but in a more specialized area or at a higher level, or in a different career completely.

It is important to know what you want to do before you start telling others to give you a job. Let's role play. You ask for a job in electrical engineering. I say, "Great! What do you do?" You say, "I am an electrical engineer." I say, "Okay, but what area is your specialty?" You say, "It does not matter. The principles are the same for all electrical engineering."

I hear the same type of story from finance, HR, and other functions. None of them are true. For CFOs you have operational oriented, accounting oriented, SEC oriented, mergers and acquisitions oriented, treasury oriented, and so on. You have CFOs who want a fast-growing company (innovative) and others who want steady growth (maintenance). You have service industries, manufacturing, securities, resale, distribution, government, and so on.

If you cannot tell me your vision of what you want to do, don't ask me to tell you. I am not your mother or father. I am looking for a grown-up to hire.

Brand

Once you know your vision, you need to determine how to communicate who you are.

Whether we like it or not, we all have a brand. Few are memorable. Most brands are forgettable. Most employees I know do not even know what their brand is.

Businesses spend millions of dollars on branding. Some brands are worth billions of dollars. Why? Because they communicate simply what the product is and the value the product has everywhere you find it.

In our case, we are the brand. Our dress, our speech, our mannerisms, our integrity, our skills, our enthusiasm, our knowledge, our experience, and our demonstrated values – all of these make up who we are. The problem is that most of us have never taken the time to reflect on who we are, where we wish to go, and what we are looking for. We just go on reacting to situations.

In developing a good brand you have to understand what you are passionate about and how you wish to take that passion into a vision. Then you have to decide what image you need that communicates your passion and vision to others.

Once you understand how to communicate your image, that becomes your brand.

Why go through all these steps? Because if you begin calling your friends and networking for help right now, it is highly likely that the first impression will be muddled and not what you want. In most towns, first impressions are all you get. The word gets around. You want to be sure the impression that gets around is the one that fits you, your passion, and your vision.

Value Proposition

A brand communicates who you are. A value proposition communicates what you can do for me. That could be targeted to a prospective employer or a sales prospect. Obviously, the brand and value proposition need to be in sync.

Many companies spend additional millions on what is called a tagline. A tagline is usually five or fewer words that communicate at a very high level what value the brand provides to them.

Let's take a test. Pretend I am a CEO in a networking meeting. I have work problems on my mind. I have people I want to meet for my benefit. I may have family issues going on at home. As a man, I usually can only focus on three things at once.

You come up to me and say, "Hi! My name is Sam." The reality is, I really only care if Sam can do something for me.

Sounds rather selfish? Sure, but I only have so much time. Maybe I want to help others – I am a nice guy, but you better catch my attention quickly. If not, my mind will wander. You have five seconds. What will you say that will make me want to listen more, for another five to ten seconds?

Your five seconds are your chance to share your value proposition, which is another way of saying something that catches my attention for my use or that a friend of mine might be interested in hearing about.

Most corporate executives I know, especially in finance, human resources, technology, and engineering, want to take five to ten minutes pouring out something. When I say "something" it is because they lost my concentration after the first five to ten seconds. After talking to twenty or more people at a networking event, I do not remember anything that most people told me. If I am fortunate, I may remember one or two people who I may be remotely interested in meeting with privately.

Unless you have passion, a vision, a brand, and a value proposition, the odds of you being that one person is low — very low. Oh, by the way, you will probably not notice that I am uninterested. I work on my presence. You just will not hear back from me.

If you cannot clearly articulate your value, don't think that I will do it for you.

Picture a London fog on the ground. Most people are in the fog and are indistinct from one another. I can tell there is someone standing there, but I don't know who it is. What passion, brand, and value propositions do is help you come out of the fog and be noticed.

Three Stories (Illustrations)

The goal of the value proposition is to support your brand and also to raise a question in my mind. If the value proposition is of interest, it should beg a question from me. You want me to ask a question for elaboration. My question indicates that I am thinking about your statement (not something else) and that I am interested in learning more. It is highly likely that my question will be to ask for further clarification of what you said. Usually my question is best answered by a short statement that gives a concrete example I can relate to. If my nonverbal expression warrants it, or if I ask for more information, you should be ready to elaborate further. Your goal is to have a dialogue, with me asking questions and you telling me your story with an illustration that supports your value proposition. If the story is interesting and relates to my interests, I will probably remember the story – and you.

Note Well: *Great communicators illustrate with stories.*

Why three stories? Because in a dialogue you never know what question you may be asked. You also may need to give several different examples.

The key is to be conversational, natural, and to use short stories. Each story must be dialogue oriented, not a monologue. Otherwise my brain may easily disengage while you stand there thinking you are successfully communicating. You may have just wasted time for both of us.

Marketing Plan

Regardless of your marketing plan, all the work we just reviewed will come in handy. Even if you run straight for a job interview, being able to communicate who you are and use stories to prove it will set you far ahead of most interviewees.

A marketing plan is critical during a transition period (looking for work). You only have so much time each day. You want to get the next job. You do not want to waste time doing activities that are not the highest return for the investment of your time. That means you need a plan. Since you are trying to sell who you are to buyers of your skills, you need a marketing plan.

So what is a marketing plan? In the context of looking for a job, it is an action plan designed to focus your time and energy and to measure progress.

Most job seekers I meet want to write their resume, blast their resume to recruiters, and wait for the calls to go interview. It does happen–I am told about 5 percent of the time.

Contingency recruiters, retained recruiters, and Internet job sites apparently represent less than 20 percent of the jobs placed in America today. My guess is that the higher the job level, the fewer the jobs that will be placed through these sources.

Therein lies the challenge. Most books talk about recruiters and how to woo them. I still recommend these books, but I advise that if at best 20 percent of success is found through recruiters or Internet job boards then 20 percent or less of your time should be in this direction.

Where does the primary focus need to be placed? At least 80 percent of success (more with higher-level jobs) is through networking.

You need to decide what your goals are, how much time to allocate to them, and what resources you need to maximize success.

Networking

Eighty percent or more of new jobs are found through networking. So the question is, How often do you network? How effective are you at networking?

Most books tell you how to write a resume or woo recruiters. Good skills, but only a fraction of what you need to know. Actually, if over 80 percent of jobs are through networking, why would resume writers and recruiters write about it? Then you may not give them a call!

As we alluded to earlier, the key to networking is 1) knowing your message, 2) knowing your goals, and 3) practice, practice, practice.

We discussed knowing your message. Knowing your goals is simple: make new friends, spread your brand and value proposition around the business community, and get one-to-one meetings with people who either have open jobs or can help refer you to their friends who may have open jobs. I strongly recommend these goals in that order. Seeking a job first makes you look desperate and lowers your market value.

Knowing how to network and getting out to do it will put you far ahead of most of your competition.

Just as important is that these skills are the same skills, when applied in the workplace, that will help you climb the ladder much faster and leave others in the dust. This is true even if others are better work performers than you. What you will be learning is how to relate to people at their level, how to communicate in their language, and how to enjoy making friends.

You spend more time at the office than with your spouse. Hiring managers want to be surrounded with friends whom they can trust and enjoy, not just good performers.

Networking skills and practice are the number one focus for winning marketing plans – after you have developed your brand, value proposition, and stories.

Marketing Document

Marketing documents were created by outplacement companies. I do not know whom to credit, but I am merely passing on their wisdom with a twist.

What is a marketing document? It is a tool that serves two purposes. First, it helps you to put down on one page your brand, value, top three supporting points, key attributes, what you are looking for, and companies you have targeted for requesting referrals into key executives. Second, it is a leave-behind tool for one-to-one meetings with friends and networking referrals so they can help you.

The second point is worth repeating: the marketing document is a tool for you to help the person you are meeting with to help you. One more time: "Help them help you."

Just as we talked about in the networking event, top executives have a lot on their plate. Time is short. Pressures seem to grow every year. When they give you time, they usually do so as an act of kindness or because they have some level of interest in you. So use your time wisely. The marketing document helps structure that time.

I strongly recommend not sharing the document until near the end of the meeting. I find eye-to-eye communication is far more valuable in developing the relationship and gaining trust. Remember, if you are going to ask for a job or a referral, then trust is the first barrier to overcome. Also, by developing a relationship you will be remembered as someone who shines above less skilled interviewees.

The contents of the first half of the document should have been discussed verbally and only serve as a reminder to the interviewer. This portion becomes a marketing brochure that the interviewer can use if he calls someone on your behalf as a referral. Referrals into decision makers and hiring managers is how you get around gatekeepers. Most gatekeepers try but often do not even know what to look for in a job opening, much less how to identify a top candidate that should be hired even when the job does not yet exist!

The list of companies you are looking into is designed to trigger the thoughts of the interviewer. Keep in mind that if you ask someone which company you should look at for a job, the interviewer will probably have a brain freeze. You need to help them. By providing a list, you are telling him the type of company and the names of companies you are pursuing. This will often trigger his memory of people who may be executives in those companies or even companies and executives not on your list but triggered by the names on the list.

Your goal is to continue making friends, to see how you can help them, and to get advice and referrals to others – without having to overtly ask. Your marketing document is a tool to accomplish that process.

Referrals

Referrals are gold. Good referrals are a reflection on the one doing the referral. His name, brand, and credibility are on the line. If you do well, you honor the referee. They will usually get feedback from the one he referred you to – often personal friends. If you do poorly, you dishonor the referee, damage your brand, and may never get another referral from him again.

Why are referrals gold? Because they indicate someone else's trust in you. This results in the referral trusting you far more than a cold call or walk-in. Keep in mind that this trust is really trust in his friend, not you. You have to prove your own trustworthiness. They are gold because they get you in front of executives whom you might never have gotten in front of any other way. They open the door. You have to earn the right to keep the door open.

Also, the referral suggests that you are as qualified a person and as competent an executive as your brand suggests you are. Thus you enter as a peer or a friend of a friend, not a groveling subordinate. Of course, you can still grovel, but you only destroy the credibility you worked so hard to achieve. Naturally, if you later prove not to be the competent executive you portrayed, you may wish to move to a different city or industry. Be honest but not sniveling. If you are good, display humble confidence appropriate for the position you are seeking.

<u>Resume</u>

Wait! Why didn't we start with the resume? Most people do! Because until this stage I personally believe you really don't know how to properly write one. In most cases, you don't need a resume until now. The marketing document should suffice.

Now you should be getting close to a job interview. Either the interviewer will ask for the resume or HR will ask for the resume. Ideally, you will have had time to tailor the resume to the company and the terms HR is looking for in their qualification checklist.

Let's take a brief look. Most of us with twenty or more years of experience can write a resume that has ten or more pages, especially overachievers. Good. Do it. We will use it for a variety of purposes but never to give to a company. Two pages is the maximum for HR or hiring managers regardless of what other authors may say.

We write the long version because we then can list all the key successes and quantified results. You will be amazed how many achievements you had over the years. You may also be disappointed that you never kept track and quantified some of your most important contributions – a mistake I hope you will never make again!

Most resumes look back in time. They "prove" that you can do what you say you can do.

The issue is that you are not interviewing to do a job that you did five years ago. You are trying to build upon your background for the job you want to do in the future. This ties to your passion, brand, and value proposition. Therefore, it is critical that you write the resume to tie to your brand and value with the history validating where you are going. If you have not developed your brand and value statement, you are really not ready to write your resume. That is, unless you want the same work and level that you had before.

<u>Interviewing</u>

Many books are written on interviewing. I am only trying to supplement them. You should not be interviewing for a job. You should be interviewing to see if the horse and saddle are the ones you really want to ride. If you fall off that horse, it is harder to get on the next one. You want to be in a position to like the horse until *you* decide to change horses.

Therefore, half of the interview should be them finding out about you. Half of the interview should be you asking questions to find out information, not publicly available, about them. Then both parties should see if there is a fit. I cannot tell you how many stories I know, including my own, about companies that misrepresented themselves in the interview process. You need to learn to look at the horse's teeth, legs, and overall health before committing your family's future on their success. Even then, there will be surprises.

So how do you prepare for the interview? The most successful executives I know may spend forty hours preparing to interview in a company. They learn what the company says their challenges are, what public information analysis suggests challenges are, and how their capabilities can help solve these challenges. This information is where you now structure your comments as to how you can help them (personally) and add value to the company.

This method moves the focus from a job specification to a series of questions and answers from both sides that becomes a dialogue. You will be amazed at what you can learn. Your intelligent questions will amaze the interviewer. Your goal, after you leave, is for the interviewer to tell his boss, "Wow! That guy is good!"

Of course, you may lose some job opportunities if you are too good. But why would you want those jobs anyway?

Negotiations

Again, there are numerous books on job or employee contract negotiations. I will not try to rehash their comments.

Consider everything potentially negotiable. The stronger your brand and value proposition, the stronger your negotiating position will be in their eyes. On the other hand, be careful not to get carried away.

The higher the level of job, the more focus you need to have in this area. I recommend working with a job negotiations specialist and/or a labor attorney. It is worth every penny.

I know a number of people who negotiated in good faith but had a downsizing, acquisition, or other event result in their being on the street. Those with good contracts have seen huge profit gains which either paid for their transition time or were put into investments for their future.

If you are at a high level, do not slight this area. Start strong. Be prepared. Hope for the best but be protected for the worst. Assume that you will be on the street before your contract expires.

If you are at a lower level, you may not be eligible for an employment contract, but you still can get terms and conditions that you might not have if you did not ask. Plus, you will be learning the ropes for when you are eligible for a contract.

Landed – Next Steps

Here is where I see the biggest mistake. Most outstanding performers cannot wait to get back into the saddle and ride into the sunset. They land and go to work. They work hard and put in long hours. I never see them again at networking events until they are in transition again. That may be as long as two to three years later. The problem is that today's horses usually only take you part of the way to your dreamed sunset.

In today's environment, there are no more careers. Let me repeat that. Today, everyone is really a contract worker (with or without a formal contract). Companies change, mentors leave, environments change, and soon you are looking for your next contract.

Another way of looking at today's marketplace is as a consultant. A consultant who works hard without looking for his next consulting assignment usually starves between assignments. He has to continue his branding, value proposition, and networking to ensure he will always have work on the horizon.

If you imitate successful consultants, you will find that they take only those jobs that fit their passion, vision, and growth in value to the next client. If you are not a fit, help refer someone else who does fit. It feels good to help others, and it raises your own brand value.

You should continue honing your skills and value inside the company and outside the company. You should continue to grow your network of friends. If you help others be successful, they will more likely be glad to help you in the future. This is a lifetime skill.

Landing is merely a step to fund the next step. Being "whacked again" could be the best thing that ever happened to you. What you do about it and what your future looks like is up to you.

The Choice Is Yours

At this point you will either be exhausted and put the book down or be excited and want to learn how to be successful in today's changing world.

This process will take time. It will take effort. It will require changing your view of what is required to succeed. Our parents did not have to make this choice. The top people before us used these techniques. Now the changing world leaves most of us little choice – unless you are willing to lower your lifestyle or not look at the future with high expectation and excitement. The choice is yours.

Chapter Two

Step One: Finding Your Passion and Creating Your Vision

Discovering Yourself – Who Are You?

The first step is often the hardest. We usually are so busy that we seldom take time to reflect on what we really want to do. Instead, we often grab the next opportunity to move up the ladder and make more money. Then, twenty years later, we discover that we are not really enjoying our life, our work, or our environment.

We know something is wrong, but we are so used to the fire drill of activity that we become desperate to get back into the routine. We merely want to get back into the same saddle we fell off the last time. That is when we look like job beggars. Not a pretty picture.

So who are we?

Are we a fabulous sales executive who enjoys the thrill of closing a deal but took a wrong turn into sales management or marketing?

Are we an operational manufacturing CFO who loves detail and efficiency but now works in a services industry or a town that lost manufacturing to China?

Are we a great number two person whose mentors retired?

Are we a great specialist who got caught in an outdated or too narrow field?

The real answer is, we are none of these things. Those items are the past. If you decide what your passion is, now is the time to look to the future. The past can predict the future, reveal a career misstep, or be a building block for your future. Which is it for you?

Hopefully, your passion builds upon your work history. That is the assumption we will be making in this book. That is why the subtitle of this book is "Secrets to Getting Back on the Executive Saddle."

If you wish to change horses, keep reading because much of the material will apply to you but you may also wish to purchase *Whacked No More! Secrets to Owning Your Own Stable©*. That will be my next book! In the meantime, consider getting "Back on the Executive Saddle" until you can plan to own your own stable of horses.

What Are Your Passions?

Why take the time to find your "passion"? Because if you don't, who will?

Most of us were dreamers as children.

I used to want to be Superman. I even had a cape (a towel) to prove it! My brother and I used to jump off our single story roof and roll when we hit the ground. I was probably five years old and was terribly disappointed that I did not fly!

As I got older I knew that I wanted to make money. A lot of money! I did not know how I was going to make my mountain of gold. I assumed that getting a college degree and working hard would do it. Compared to 95 percent of Americans, I cannot complain.

Most of you reading this book have also succeeded but somehow were "whacked" along the way. Now you may be finding that you are older, the competition is fierce, and somehow getting back in the saddle is difficult. Times have changed.

Some of you may be much younger and earlier in your career. You may not even have been "whacked" yet! Congratulations! If you follow these steps, you will be further ahead than most of your peers. You will probably also succeed and, potentially, rise further than most of us.

So what is the key to discovering your passion?

Write down a list of what excites you to want to jump out of bed each day. Do it now.

Have a list of five to ten areas? If so, you may be a master of none – a wannabe. Some of you may list none, nada, zip, the big zero. Don't worry; most people would not know what to say either. We are too busy pursuing daily life and trying to survive to even dream that we could discover our passion and then pursue it!

Now, let's review what you have. If your list is zero, we will come back to you. If you have five to ten areas, you may be a great thinker and excited about various topics. Let's examine typical examples:

➢ Great spouse and parent	Hopefully we all have that passion!
➢ Great man/woman of God	Can anyone argue that?
➢ Pro golfer	Is your handicap in negative numbers?
➢ Pro fisherman	Do you have a room full of trophies?
➢ Maker of wood boats	Have you done it before?
➢ Writer of books	Will people pay to read your work?

➤ Public speaker	What topic? What is your feedback?
➤ Cold-calling salesman	Congratulations; you are weird but valuable!
➤ M&A work	Like pressure and the "deal'"?
➤ Operations	Like taking an idea and making it work?
➤ Creating new industries	I know. Who would be crazy enough…
➤ Helping others find work	"Paying it forward" can make a difference
➤ Hard-relationship sales	"Easy" means wine and dining – I could do that! If I could find a $200k job like that…

Now let's take a pulse. No, the patient is dead. I do not see your list.

So let's take my list. Great husband, father, man of God, public speaking, helping others find work, and creating new industries would be on my list. Okay, I like a challenge!

No one is standing in line to pay me as a husband, father, or man of God. These things are my personal passions and personal values. On the other hand, if you want to contribute, call me and I will tell you where to send the check!

The way I play golf or fish, I can guarantee that I have to pay others to let me participate. Unless you are on the circuit now, there's a good chance that these are hobbies.

I do speak publicly on several topics. How can I get Bill Clinton-size gigs? In the meantime, I speak for lesser sums and to create leads for my core business.

Helping others find ways of getting work might be interesting. I could even be crazy enough to write a book! As we will see later, if helping others is not on your list it should be. Most successful people have mentors and helpers and are interested in helping others. We will talk about this gold mine later, but unless you wish to be a recruiter or outplacement specialist, you may need to add another item that others might be willing to actually pay you to do!

If you love cold calling, call me! I need you. So do most companies. You should have no problem finding work.

If you love mergers and acquisitions (high-paced action) in a future high-growth industry, then write that down in bold, italics, and 32-point font size.

If you love operational change improvements, you have a large peer group and will need to refine what operations and changes excite you the most.

If you love relationship sales in an installed base with a huge brand name behind you, better hope you are not too old. Order takers are a dying breed in most industries.

If you love networking and business development, solutions selling, and umbrella relationship sales, then write that down in bold, italics, and 48-point font size.

We will take as examples the mergers and acquisitions (M&A), operational, and business development passions as examples to expand our future discussions.

The key is, what is on your list?

If I told you that, due to circumstances beyond your control, you will never be able to afford to retire, what would you want to do to earn a living for the rest of your life?

If you are age fifty, that could be thirty-five years of doing what you enjoy or hating each day. The decision is up to you.

Today, no one is "owed" a high-paying job. Hard workers are often left on the lower rungs of the ladder. Past success does not guarantee a job tomorrow. Now is the time to decide what you want to do for the rest of your life.

If you can align what makes you want to jump out of bed every morning, what you are really good at doing, and what fits the lifestyle you want, then you will be excited at your future. Once you know who you are and what your passions are, your excitement will be contagious! If your passions match those of employers, they will want to get to know you – and hire you. And that is the point I am trying to make.

Which Passion Is Marketable?

You may have a passion for home mortgage lending. If you find yourself at a major downturn in the market, that may not be the best saddle to get back on for a few years.

Perhaps commercial lending, workouts, or developing a market helping distressed owners survive in a downturn might be viable ways to stay in your industry and thrive until the next upswing.

Look at trends in your field. If they are positive, great! If work is moving to China or demand is disappearing, it is time to reassess where your talents can be applied to a growth area.

To illustrate, imagine that you are a buggy whip manufacturing executive. You may have a problem making six figures today. By examining your understanding of leather and design, you might be able to move into automobile seat design and be the one outsourcing the production to China. Perhaps you can open a specialized Internet opportunity for high-quality (i.e. expensive) purses or perhaps leather goods for polo players. It would not take many $7,000 purses that you could sell on the Web worldwide to make six figures.

Hopefully, your situation and trend analysis will require less creativity. For the sake of our discussions, we will take the previous passions and assume there are plenty of positions where you could land if you can break through the challenges of getting back in the saddle.

Translating Passion into Vision

The first challenge is to translate your passion into a specific vision.

What is vision? Take a mental picture of where you would like to work. What does it look like? What is the environment? How much travel is involved? How much income is required? What is your market worth? What is your picture?

Let's take and apply some examples.

Example 1: Mergers and Acquisitions

Are you the VC investor, CFO, CEO, CTO/CIO, HR, or a support person wanting to eventually enter the "C-Suite"? Let's take the CFO. Do you have prior experience in M&A? If so, is it with similar-size companies, similar industries, and similar technologies? How extensive is your banking or treasury experience? How much money would you require? Would you be willing to sit underneath a more experienced executive to learn from them? Does laying off "good" people to make the new company meet expectations bother you? Are you willing to travel extensively to raise funds, to visit plants, or to optimize units? Are you willing to put in long hours, missing many key family moments?

What skills, abilities, experiences, network, and solutions can you bring to the party? How well can you work with an M&A team? How well do you dress? Do you spend time on your appearance? Do you drive a stylish car?

Are you Sarbanes Oxley knowledgeable, a CPA, and an experienced "A" player?

Are you a visionary? Can you see the whole picture? Do you get excited about doing deals, optimizing organizations, implementing IT solutions, and merging financials?

What does your picture look like?

Example 2: Operations

Are you the CEO, CFO, CTO, HR, or a support person wanting to run a small operating company or a director/VP wanting to run an operational division? What size company do you feel comfortable in?

Note: If you are a Fortune 500 person over fifty years of age, you may have a higher chance of success in a $50-$500 million company or division.

What industries are reflected in your background? What industry would you "die" to be in?

What type of operations would you prefer? Are you one who likes to be a world-class change agent or a "keep the business running" guy?

Do you like traditional manufacturing and distribution? Or do you prefer outsourcing globally in a Web-based highly customized, quick-turnaround, low-cost environment? Or do you prefer a financial services industry where technology is king, customer service is a challenge, and economic cycles and legislation can harm or benefit? Or do you prefer a consulting, legal, medical, engineering, or other services industry?

Do you have prior experience in operations? If so, is it with similar-size companies, similar industries, and similar technologies? How extensive is your technology experience (Great Plains, SAP, Oracle, etc.)? How much money would you require? Would you be willing to sit underneath a more experienced executive to learn from them in a new industry? Does laying off "good" people to make the new company meet expectations bother you? Are you willing to travel extensively to visit plants, participate in endless meetings, and optimize units? Are you willing to put in long hours, missing many key family moments?

What skills, abilities, experiences, network, and solutions can you bring to the party? How well can you work with an operational team? How well can you work with "corporate" guidelines and "unrealistic expectations"? How well do you dress? Do you spend time on your appearance? Do you drive an efficient and reliable car?

Are you a learner? Do you get excited about brainstorming, best practices, quality, motivating teams to be more efficient, lowering cost, and improving internal and external customer service?

What does your picture look like?

Example 3: Business Development

Are you the whiz bang sales consultant? Are you the master networking and relationship guru? Do you thrive on selling complex solutions that bring value, economics, and competitive advantage to clients?

What industries are reflected in your background? What industry would you "die" to be in? What industries would love to have you? In sales, industry experience can be more critical than in operations or "C-Suite" jobs. A sales engineer selling steel fabrication trying to move into Fortune 500 software solution sales may be a stretch. On the other hand, a sales engineer selling construction services for commercial properties may be believable, as long as he does not try to pretend to understand foundation engineering!

Can you define yourself as a sales guy rather than a sales engineer? Of course you can! What would that picture look like to you?

What type of sales would you prefer? Are you the one who likes to be the Fortune 500 consulting business development VP or the one selling medical devices into hospitals?

What prior sales experience do you have? What kind of sales training have you been through? Are you strong enough to realize that most sales training is not appropriate for every company or industry? How extensive is your technology experience (Great Plains, SAP, Oracle, etc.), medical experience, "C-Suite and Board" selling experience, plant floor selling experience…?

How much money would you require? How open are you to a low fixed salary with high variable commissions? How do you feel about total compensation capping (when the CEO does not allow sales to make more than him)?

Are you willing to travel extensively to visit prospects, clients, networking events, and global locations; participate in endless meetings; and have productive airport wait times? Are you willing to put in long hours, missing many key family moments?

What skills, abilities, experiences, network, and solutions can you bring to the party? How well can you work with an operational team? How well can you work with "corporate" guidelines and "unrealistic expectations"? How well do you dress? Do you spend time on your appearance? Do you drive an efficient and reliable car, a luxury car, or a sports car?

Are you a learner? Do you get excited about brainstorming, best practices, quality, motivating teams to be more efficient, lower cost, and higher internal and external customer service? Are you focused on customer success, your employer's success, or your personal success? Do you thrive on "win-win" or "eating the young"?

What does your picture look like?

You need to write down your vision. There will be many companies that fit your vision. The key is how to find them and communicate to them that you "fit their culture." If you cannot frame your passion into a vision that you can paint for someone else, neither will they paint it for you.

A note of caution to sales executives: You may be tempted to bypass this exercise. Don't. You may be used to selling products with brochures, marketing support, and product management support. Now you are the product. What we are talking about is the way you develop your own brochures, marketing, and product management with you as the product. This may be harder than you think, but most of your competition will not make the effort. Be the exception. Be the exception and move ahead of the pack.

Chapter Three

Step Two: Creating Your Brand

ᐱᑎ

Before I begin, I wish to recognize that many of these branding concepts are from Jim Lynch of Lynchpin Associates, a brand-marketing consultancy based in Atlanta. Jim's career in branding was instrumental in working with Coke and UPS branding. Thank you for teaching me about branding, Jim!

What Is the Value of a Brand?

Here is an amazing fact. The value of each top brand is worth *billions* of dollars. Coke has the highest brand value year after year – worth *tens of billions* of dollars. The top 100 brands are like a who's who of names you have heard of and have a good feeling about.

Here is an application for us. What is your brand worth? You probably never thought of yourself as a brand, but you are either a commodity brand or a specialist brand or a very high-value and sought-after brand. Which would you like to be seen as by hiring managers? Think your brand may influence your getting the job, getting top dollar, getting perks, and getting future opportunity? You bet.

So what is your brand worth?

None of the major consumer brands takes branding lightly. They invest significantly in maintaining and expanding their brand value. That means that branding value can grow. So can you and your brand.

Before we explore how to brand yourself, let's look at what a brand is.

What Is a Brand?

A brand contains four elements: recognized phrase, visual symbol, emotional tie, and image perception. Let's examine each.

<u>Recognized Phrase</u>

Coke is the most recognized name in the world. You can travel to almost any country and ask for a "Coke" – and get a Coke. Quality, taste, and satisfaction (results) are the same worldwide.

UPS is not merely a company name; it is a brand that exhibits global delivery of packages in brown trucks, brown jets, and brown-uniformed employees. When it comes to parcel package deliveries, you think of UPS.

FedEx has a name that labeled a service. When you "FedEx" a package you mean overnight, even though UPS and DHL also offer overnight services.

Ever make photocopies? Xerox invented the concept and for years people would say, "Please Xerox this for me."

What is in a name? Perceived value, repeatable performance, and reliable results tied to a name means that when you wish to buy, the brand name is the first to come to mind.

Wouldn't it be nice if the hiring manager, wishing to buy (hire), first thought of you?

Would that be of value to you?

The key to a recognized phrase is that it is simple, memorable, and descriptive of you.

This is very hard to do. Companies spend millions every year trying to develop their name recognition in the marketplace.

A friend of mine says he is a "spaceman." He is a commercial realty buyer's agent. Once he explains what he does, you may never forget him as the "spaceman" (guy who helps you find commercial *space).* Of course, he may not wish to announce that to a psychiatrist!

So what is your recognizable phrase?

For my business, IEM, I constantly struggle with the best phrase. I keep experimenting and one day will find something that "zings." For now, IEM stands for a new industry called Indirect Expense Management. The brand is both IEM and "the expense management experts." We will come back to this area in the discussion on value proposition.

Keep in mind, brands are often higher valued and priced products. Don't you deserve to be of higher value (price) than others who never developed their brand and are being treated as a mere commodity? If the shopper just wants a commodity, let them go elsewhere. Your brand name has value – if you take the time to develop it.

Visible Symbol

For Coke, the symbol is their name and the script font of Coke or Coca-Cola. For UPS, it is the phrase "brown" and their logo, which is found on their trucks, uniforms, and everywhere you look. The symbol represents the product and its reputation.

For someone trying to get back in the saddle, you should consider your visible image.

You may have heard the phrases: "Clothes make the individual," "He looks sharp," "Look at what he drives," "He goes to church at...," "He lives in the ...neighborhood."

You get the picture. Image counts. Remember, first impressions may be your last impression. Be sure it is a good impression.

Image also has to be managed. Let's take each of the above examples and comment on them.

"Clothes make the individual"

There really is a "dress for success" paradigm that creates part of your image. I still struggle with it. If you need a graphic example, you may wish to watch the TLC television show *What Not to Wear*. The focus is usually on women's wear but the concepts point out several rules which I have expanded upon.

Rule One: Never go outside the house dressed in an outfit that may create confusion about your brand. Most of us like to dress very comfortably (spelled frumpy). That is fine if your brand is the city frump.

Rule Two: Determine your appropriate brand clothing image. If you are a successful lawyer or doctor, your appearance in a tuxedo to mow the lawn may not be appropriate. Sandals, cut-off jeans, and a "wife-beater" undershirt may also not be appropriate. What you wear to the office or to the grocery store should be thought out as part of your brand.

Different parts of the country have different cultures and definitions as to what is appropriate for the image.

I struggle with this because I hate to buy clothes or spend money on clothes. My motto is, "If it can last twenty years, let's wear it until the holes get too big!" For most of us, our dress will be a work in progress.

Rule Three: Dress within your financial ability. Ever see someone who buys Armani but can only afford Wrangler? Believe me, you will fool no one very long.

Rule Four: Get help. The first person who helps me is my wife. I totally trust her and depend upon her. If you need help, an image consultant will cost money but is well worth it.

Rule Five: Consider your clothes as an investment. Choose them as carefully as you would an investment. Is the return on your investment worth the cost?

Rule Six: Do not buy too many clothes. Basics, with proper matching, go a long way. It is too easy to go overboard and have a closet that is full of clothes, shoes, or hats that you never wear.

Rule Seven: Proper clothing can make you feel great! Take the time to dress right. The feeling of confidence and your inner smile become the most important reflection of your image and brand.

"He looks sharp"

Ever notice how men and women whom society pictures as "beautiful, cute, sexy, or handsome" seem to be very successful? A study even suggested that tall men are more successful than average-sized men. Whether we like it or not, our looks matter.

I am not suggesting plastic surgery (unless you are disfigured) or buying platform shoes (unless an orthopedic doctor recommends them for a limp). I am suggesting that you take a close look in the mirror and videotape yourself standing and sitting. If you are like me, you will see years' worth of improvement opportunities!

Let's take a look at some considerations:

For Men:

- Do you have comb-over hair? In other words, if you are balding, do you just let one side grow longer and flip it over the top to cover your baldness?

  Don't be bashful. I had comb-over hair for years. I told you I was a work in progress! When you see my picture now, you will see my baldness. At least I am genuine. I also don't have to blow-dry my hair as long.

  I have been told that "bald is beautiful" and "bald is sexy." I like that. I have also been told that God only made so many perfect heads, and the rest He covered with hair. I like that even better!

- Do you have facial hair? I wore a mustache for thirty-five years. My wife only saw me once without my mustache. That was on our wedding day. I had shaven it off to please her. She asked me to grow it back because, at my age of twenty-four, it made our wedding pictures look like she married a child!

  Last year, an image consultant brought me up in front of high-level executives to point out that 95 percent of men should not wear facial hair. That included me. So I shaved it off and have kept it off. My wife now likes me without the mustache. My clean-shaven face makes it look like she married a younger man!

  This is big: If you are older and looking for a job, looking younger might be a good thing.

For Women:

- Consider going to a makeup expert. It is amazing how makeup can transform a woman. It is also amazing how inexpensive or improperly applied makeup can make a woman look cheap, sleazy, old, and, well, sad. My wife is beautiful and her new makeup makes her feel even better about herself. That glow shows. She is worth the investment.

- Consider going to a top-notch hair salon. We have all seen amazingly bad hairdos. Perhaps you cannot afford a routine cut at a top salon, but one visit to find the best style and color for you can be invaluable. If you have ever watched *What Not to Wear*, the makeup and hair improvements seem to be more transforming than even the clothes.

   Husbands, encourage your wives. The investment will pay dividends.

- Although the next comment could also be under "clothing," *never* dress with necklines too low, clothing too tight, or dresses too high. You may think that these habits are sexy and fun. They only attract the wrong kind of attention. They are distracting to top-level professionals. They only lower your brand and usually eliminate you from any serious contention for top-level jobs.

   You may "look good," but men will just be enjoying the view, other women might become jealous, and *nobody* will take you seriously.

For Both Men and Women:

- Look at your weight and physical conditioning. This is probably one of the hardest areas to change. Life is busy. Life can be hard. Going to school, raising a family, and working leaves little time for anything else, including exercise.

   Have you ever watched *The Biggest Loser* on NBC? Talk about inspirational!

They say 90 percent of those who lose weight will gain it all back, and more. Most exercise equipment winds up being expensive clothing hangers.

If you looked at my goals for next year, they include losing weight and gaining tone. I think 99 percent of the rest of America has made the same resolution.

However, how many top executives do you see with a weight problem?

Being overweight does not mean you have a questionable character. It might mean that you have emotional issues, control issues, health issues, life-expectancy issues, and appearance issues. It also means that you may not be visually appealing as "one of the club members." Either way, it does impact your brand and ability to compete in a challenging job market.

If you do have the appropriate weight (not too much or too little), you will also be healthier, have more energy, and feel better about yourself – all which impacts your brand.

- Look at your diet. Oh, there he goes again talking about weight! Yes and no. Yes, because the discussion above applies and diet is the other half of exercise.

No, because I am referring to what you eat, where, and with whom. Let's talk about some examples.

First, if you are in San Francisco, a vegan diet is acceptable. A steak diet may be "politically incorrect." If you are in Kansas, a medium rare (or raw), cornfed steak is what "real men" eat. If you are in Atlanta, it does not seem to matter.

"Look at what he drives"

This area is more difficult. Decisions can be very expensive, even budget breaking. The best decision is not always the most expensive car. The question is, what image are you trying to make?

For me, cars are utilitarian. I always bought my wife the new car and took the old car until it was falling apart. That was good for economics but bad for business, for image, and for long-term image economics.

I am now a CEO and drive a nice black Lexus. I bought it recently used and do not plan to trade the car in for a few years. My personal model is expensive but as inexpensive as reasonable for my position.

The answer is not always expensive. We have a friend who is extremely successful in landscaping. His minimum project costs over $300,000. He lives in a very nice house with acreage on a hill in the country. He owns nice cars and a helicopter. Yet, when he goes to prospective clients' homes to sell his high-end landscaping solutions, he drives an old beat-up station wagon. He is not intending to be deceptive but neither does he want the prospective client to think he is overpaying for his landscaping. From the amount of awards his company receives, his clients are getting a good deal – and feel good about the cost.

So what is the best car for you? You will often see top-of-the-line sedans for CEOs, sports cars for top salespeople, more practical cars for CFOs and finance, and trucks for good old boys or those working in the field. Take a look at what people drive in the position you aspire to get to see if you can picture (and afford) yourself in that model.

"He goes to church at..."

This could also be the synagogue, temple, or other religious facility that is socially prestigious.

Today this area is less significant than it used to be. America appears to be rapidly moving to a secular society.

In my case, I am very active in a fantastic church that also happens to be large and wealthy. Many people go to such churches to network. I do not. I go because that is where I feel led to go.

Because this area appears to be less important today, hopefully the hypocrisy level will decrease. In my personal opinion, if you are going to church, synagogue, or temple to network and be "socially acceptable," then your brand is that of a user and loser.

Authenticity and integrity are marks of leaders whose impact lasts even after they pass away.

You may think differently. It is your call and your brand.

"He lives in the...neighborhood"

We happen to be privileged to live in a nice area. It is not the wealthiest or gaudiest, but it is one of the places where people with our professional goals live. That means we are consistent in where we live with what we do. Our brand is authentic.

Many cannot afford to live where they would like to live. Life can be hard. Frankly, good schools and low crime are more important than what the house or yard looks like.

Many wealthy people live lower than their means. That is just wise for a number of reasons. However, few top executives choose to live in the slums.

Like all branding decisions, where you live and how kept your house and lawn are should be consistent with where you are and where you want to be.

At the end of the day, be sure your symbol is what you want. There is a small book on branding called *Purple Cow* by Seth Godin. In marketing, you want to be noticed. If you are a black cow among hundreds of other black cows, you will be accepted by the other cows and look like them. If you are a purple cow, you may not be accepted by the black-cow herd but you will definitely be noticed among them!

Depending on your point of view, being a purple cow can be a good thing. You will stand out in the crowd. Just be sure that your purple cow brand is authentically you.

In my case, I want to be accepted by my clients, who often become my friends, and be noticed most for the value I bring to the table.

Remember, your visual image is part of your brand. Just as companies have a marketing budget for branding, plan to set aside some funds for your visual image. You are worth it, and the return on your investment will put a smile on your face. You will also feel more confident and worth the money you spent.

Emotional Tie

Have you noticed the commercials of a polar bear family drinking and celebrating Coke? How did it make you feel?

Did you see the Lexus Christmas commercials where a husband or wife surprises their spouse with a brand-new Lexus with a huge red bow on top?

Most advertising has an emotional appeal. Some of it plays to the base nature of sexuality, being one of the gang, envy, or a host of other emotional themes that usually have nothing to do with the product.

Most people buy with their heart, not their head.

Have you noticed that CEOs often buy from friends, even if the product is priced higher or is not quite as good? There are emotions of trust, helping, and friendship. Loyalty to fraternity brothers, golf buddies, association members, and relatives often trump what is intellectually best. In a contest of heart and mind, the heart usually wins.

This is less of a problem for most executives in finance, technology, engineering, and the sciences. We recognize that our hearts are often deceptive and lead to wrong decisions. Our minds usually tell us what is right. We often put our emotions aside and go with our minds.

Yet even the most heartless of us prefer to do business with those we believe we can trust. Trust is the balance between mind (history tells us they are trustworthy) and heart (we feel best working with those we trust).

So what applications can we apply to branding with emotional ties?

- Learn to talk in illustrations, stories, and pictures that relate to the heart. This clarifies your point, makes your point memorable, and speaks to the heart.
- Develop a reputation (brand) of being trustworthy. Poor customer service, lying, failing to set proper expectations, divulging private conversations, or stabbing *anybody* in the back can destroy everything else you try to build. If I see your failure in any of these areas, my thought is, *Will you do that to me?* I will not take that risk.
- Develop true friendships. Most wives say their husbands have no true friends. By their standards (confidant, time availability, and loyalty), I suspect wives are right. Most men have many acquaintances and very few friends.
- Smile and be positive. The world may be falling apart, but there are many wonderful and exciting things going on in the world. You should be a reason to cause others to smile and be positive in return. It is contagious.

It is often said that you have to be a friend to make a friend. As we shall see later, there is a concept called "pay it forward" that means we are willing to help others without any expectation of them paying us back. The belief is that somewhere, somehow, our efforts will help others and eventually someone else will help us.

That means when we network we should seek to help others before expecting anyone to help us. We will talk about this more in the networking section, but let me ask you this: If you came up to ask me for a job and handed me your business card, and someone else came up to me and engaged me in a dialogue, who do you think I would be more emotionally interested in helping?

If your networking and interest are sincere, most people are at least open to helping if they can. If your interest is insincere, you have just destroyed your brand.

Image Perception

You might suspect that all of the previous discussion combined together creates your image. It does, but there is more. I did not spend time talking about your speech or other image areas. For example, do you speak with a heavy accent? What kind of language do you use (word selection, sophistication, clarity, volume control, etc.)? Remember the movie *My Fair Lady?* If not, you may want to rent it. The story speaks for itself.

One final point I wish to make in this chapter: building your brand (image) is not an overnight occurrence. It is who you are at the office, at home, and when no one sees you. Inauthentic people may fool other inauthentic people. People wearing masks have a hard time seeing the other person's mask.

Building your brand happens over time overtly or by inaction. The difference is that you can decide which brand is genuine for you and then work, over time, to improve your branding. Coke and UPS did not build their brand value overnight. Neither will you.

Remember the key drivers of successful branding: recognized phrase, visual symbol, emotional tie, and image perception. The key is not to spend all your time focusing on branding—just be the best brand, for what you do, in the marketplace!

There is hope for all of us, so let's get started!

Chapter Four

Step Three: Creating Your Value Proposition

Have you ever listened to radio station WIIFM? I am told it means "What's In It For Me?"

Wait a minute! This is all about *me* (my job hunt), *me* (my family needs), *me* (my pride)! This is all about *my* work experience, *my* accomplishments, *my* education, *my* skills, *my* knowledge, *my* looks, and *my* wonderfulness!

"Oh, I am sorry. My mind wandered off. What were you saying? Oh my, look at the time. I have to go. Bye-bye." And so walks off anyone of significance who can help you.

When you are the hiring manager or the influential executive, you can brag about yourself. When you are trying to get back into the saddle, you need to communicate how you can help them – what value you bring to the hiring manager and influencers, the company, or his friends.

This is so important I will repeat it often...

Help Others Help You

The first way to help others help you is by clearly explaining value to them in a very short, memorable way.

63

Remember the discussion in branding about your "recognized phrase"? Oh, I know. That was several pages ago. I get lost too. But remember the "spaceman"?

We need to be able to state our "recognized phrase" in terms that are memorable and have value to a company or someone who can help us. The value to us is that we might be remembered, might get a networking referral, and might get a job.

Once we are hired, we need to continue our branding and honing our value statement. The need to be memorable and show value to higher-level executives, who make promotional decisions, is just as acute.

What Is Your Tagline?

Let's take a test. You have five seconds to say something about who you are and what you do that makes me want to listen more to you. Ready? Go! One. Two. Three. Four. Five. Time is up! Write down what you would say. Test it on others. Hmmm…difficult isn't it?

If your brand stands alone so that you can say one word, like "Coke," you may not need a tagline. But even Coke will say something like "The Coke side of life" or "The drink that refreshes." These are emotional appeals to bolster the "value" of the drink to you personally. My guess is that your value proposition is not quite there yet. So let's get to work.

A tagline is a phrase of a few words that says everything you need to let your audience "plug" you into their grid of understanding. The best lines have three results:

1. Tell someone what you do
2. Grab their attention and urge them to ask to know more (raise a question)
3. Have an emotional link

Okay, let's test a few that I use. Keep in mind that I am not satisfied with any of them yet.

First, for IEM, "We put money into your pocket." Does it tell you what we do? Combined with the brand "expense management experts," it suggests that we take money that does not belong to someone else and put it back into your company's pocket. Does it grab attention? Yes. Money usually gets people's attention. Does it beg a question? Yes. The usual questions are, "How?" and "What types of expenses?" Does it raise an emotional response? Yes. Usually the person I am talking to is thinking or asking, "Can you help put money into my pocket?"

Second, for identity theft, "I am the Identity Theft Guy." Does it tell you what I do? Yes, the area is identity theft. Does it grab their attention and beg for a question? I find that it does to most people. They want to know whether I am an identity theft thief or a solution provider. They want to know what I offer in that area. They want to know what I think about someone else's solution. They often want to tell me their story or a friend's story about how they were affected by identity theft. Third, it raises a deep emotional link called fear of being a victim.

If you analyze these answers, several observations occur. First, either potential clients are interested or not, but they know what I do. Second, they are engaged in a question-and-answer dialogue (perfect for them to remember me). Third, they are emotionally engaged and now view me as a subject matter expert (which I am). Mission accomplished.

Now creating a tagline is not really that easy. Most of us do a lot of different things and can offer a huge array of value to a hiring manager. That results in a number of major mistakes. Let me list two and see if you are making them.

- Your tagline lasts five minutes, not five seconds. Vomiting out your life history or a wide number of amazing abilities will have the opposite impact you intend. Your message is that you are tactical, not focused, and a generalist. The biggest issue is that when I walk away, I will probably give up trying to remember anything because you gave me too much to remember.

Don't feel bad. Most of us talk too much and have this challenge.

- Your tagline is short but includes a laundry list of things you do. Better, but I will still have a hard time remembering you.

Don't believe me? Once, when I was in high school, I was introducing my best friend of six years to other new acquaintances. I forgot his name. Call me stupid, but that has happened to many people. I wanted to remember but had a brain freeze.

Now, if I walk away from hearing your tagline and two weeks later I am playing golf with a top executive who asks me if I know someone who fits your profile, you want me to say, "Actually I met someone who may fit perfectly. His name is Sam Marvelous, and he is a great _____ guy. How about I introduce the two of you?" Bingo!

You do not want me to say, "Actually I met someone who may fit perfectly, but I cannot remember him. If he comes to mind, I will give you a call." Want to bet if you will later come to mind? You would not believe how often that happens.

The other answer is, "No, I can't think of anyone." That means you made *no* impression. Ouch.

So how do you get started?

What Is Your Unique Value?

If you say, "I am a CFO." Great! You are at the top of the heap, with at least 150,000 others in the United States. Ho-hum.

You might say, "I am a CFO with sales and general management experience in the medical device industry." It is still too many words, but now I know what you are and that you have experiences that 99 percent of other CFOs do not have. I may want to know more.

How many CFOs do you know who also have sales experience? Most CEOs with sales experience see finance as the "sales prevention department." If you are able to help both sales and finance, are you worth talking to and referring to friends? You bet!

Perhaps a better statement would be, "I am a CFO who also has sales management experience." Leave out more technical details. You can always expand but you only have seconds to frame your key value differentiations. Don't lose your point with tactical clutter.

Or you could say, "I am a CFO focusing on streamlining operations and profit improvement." Got it. What about industry? Key: Do not answer a question that has not been asked. Financial operations are similar across industries. The statement begs them to ask what industry. Their question indicates engagement. They are thinking about you. Now you can say, "I have been in financial services, consulting, and manufacturing companies and found my methods effective across industries." Guess what? You are on second base.

Now, to get to third base, you need a story. We will talk about that next.

Home plate is a meeting. We will discuss that later.

So what is your unique value? How can you say it briefly, memorably, and such that there is a reason (some benefit) for them to want to know more?

How Can You Add Unique Value That Sets You Apart From Others?

Easy! How many of your friends even know what their passion is, have a vision, are developing their brand, and have a strong value proposition/tagline?

In most cases the answer is none. If you have done the work, welcome to the front of the line. You will be more impressive, more memorable, more credible, and more valuable. We are talking about you having a competitive advantage in the marketplace.

If you do not implement these recommendations and your competitor does, then I do not have to tell you the implications. Have you ever wondered how and why others moved up the ladder faster than you? This may be a reason.

Creating Your Message

Okay. You are sold. But where do you start? Glad you asked. Here is how:

- Get out your resume in an electronic format such as Word.
- Start expanding every section, focusing on both qualitative and quantitative accomplishments. Be verbose. Write until your brains fall out. If you have over ten years of experience you should have at least ten pages (one page per year). If you do not have that many documented accomplishments, you may not be the "A" player you thought you were. Or, as some have illustrated, I hope you are not one of those who have one year's experience, twenty times. Do the best you can with what you have.
- Create a spreadsheet, such as Excel. Go back through your resume and list each accomplishment in a brief

phrase. List each type of company. List what you did to achieve the accomplishment. Include education and military results. List each industry. List each political environment. List geographies covered.

Analyze your past. Your past is a predictor of your future. If your passion, vision, and brand all support your past successes, you are on your way. If not, see if you can find support for what you wish to do in the future from what you have done in the past.

- Write out again your passion, vision, and brand.
- Now look at what you have written and answer the following questions:
  - What trends of achievements do you see?
  - Where did you outshine others?
  - When did you enjoy yourself the most? What were you doing?
  - What is it that you would like to do in the future (passion and vision)?
  - Does your passion and vision tie to what you have done in the past?
  - If so, what top achievements would best explain how you would help a future employer?
  - Of all your achievements, can you quantify the results?
  - What political environments did you enjoy?
  - What size companies did you enjoy? Why?
  - What type of job did you enjoy? Was it chaotic and fast-paced, high-growth, or baby-sitting? Why did you enjoy it?
  - What geographic locations did you enjoy? Why?
  - How much travel do you wish to do?
  - How many hours per week are you willing to work?
- Of your top ten achievements:

- Write out a short story for each achievement of what you did and what the value was to the company.
- Prioritize your achievements by impact significance.

Doing Your Research

Write out the profile of your ideal job that would fit your vision. List the size of the company, position, who you would report to, desired compensation, where the company is located, its political environment, and what the culture looks like, whether the company is fast-growing, slow-growing, troubled, a start-up, or a mature company, etc.

Now do an Internet search to find ten companies with profiles that match your profile the closest. List these companies.

For most Fortune 500 executives, getting back into the saddle in another large company is tempting but usually unlikely. Companies under $1 billion in revenue will be far easier to target. For many executives, companies ranging from $50 million to $500 million will be the best fit and offer a wider selection. For others, $10 million to $50 million might be the best fit. Consider the size of company carefully. Some of the best jobs are with smaller but growing companies.

Next research their websites, their public information, the executives, what others say about them, and what their issues might be.

After that, test your tagline and profile to see how you will persuade them that you would be a tremendous asset to their company.

Finally, locate former employees who still live in your area that you might be able to talk to over coffee.

Testing Your Brand and Value Proposition

Once you have your tagline, your message, and your research, the reality is that you will need to refine them in the marketplace.

Do they communicate clearly, with few words, the message you wish to present?

Is your brand consistent with the profile of your targeted ten companies?

Call the former employees to ask questions, walk through your brand, and share your value proposition. Ask for their input and opinions. Try to meet with them over coffee, breakfast, or lunch. They will be more relaxed than in the office. You will be amazed at what you can discover. Take every comment with a grain of salt. Former employees sometimes have hard feelings. Ask if they know someone whom they can refer you to meet.

Do you still feel too nervous and not ready to talk to these former employees? Wait a few chapters and then you should be ready.

Chapter Five

Step Four: Creating Your Stories

Create a Tree for Each Story

You know your passion. You know your vision. You know your brand. You know how your background supports your vision. You have written ten stories for major achievements that support your vision and tagline. Now it is time to structure your approach.

First, when someone asks "What do you do?" you answer with what you *want* to do – your well-crafted tagline is usually the right start.

If their eyes glaze over, either you need to work more on your tagline or they are just not interested and you respond by asking what they do. Have some small talk, but if no connection develops it is time to move on to someone else.

If their eyes brighten or they respond with a question, it is time to work your magic.

Think about a large tree. At the top you see a point (tagline) followed by smaller branches followed by gradually longer branches as you go down toward the ground. Each branch has other branches growing from it in different directions.

Martin Schmidler suggested a similar analogy with icebergs. "Above the iceberg waterline is what's most visible. By using carefully crafted sound-bites you can engage the other person. Below the waterline are the details to support your sound-bites."

Here is the concept. Once you state your tagline you will need to be able to provide one-sentence descriptions that define what you mean.

Here are two examples.

For my primary business, my brand is IEM and "expense management experts." Our tagline is "We put money into your pocket."

What am I doing? First I need to create a word picture that emotionally fits what we do and is memorable. Hopefully, I have piqued their interest for a few seconds. Now I have to be ready to build topical branches.

I can then illustrate with stories of how companies often overpay for telecom, health care, and other major expenses. I can discuss how we recover money overpaid and also reduce future losses. My stories may include percentages of cash or raw dollars. Some examples are million-dollar impacts.

I want them thinking, *How can I use this service in my company or to refer to a friend?*

Note: *The key is you have seconds and minutes—then their mind will wander.*

Each key statement must be planned and practiced for the opening. It must be brief and clear to say what you want to say. That way you are less likely to stumble and more likely to be bold in approaching others.

The next step is to be able to give examples about what we have done (stories). However, I take one step first. I ask a few questions.

Why stop my spewing to ask questions? I am looking for engagement, thinking, and dialogue. I also want to ensure I pick the stories that are most relevant to them.

So I might ask how many people are in their company, what type of business they are in, or how many locations they have. Why ask these pointed questions? Because the number of people drives costs, a law firm has different spend patterns than a manufacturing or marketing company, and multiple locations increases costs, complexity, and inefficiency.

The good news is that I have examples I can use for any of these cases that are appropriate to them and show directly how I can impact their bottom line.

The structure we are talking about can be used in networking, referral meetings, and interviewing. It looks like this:

Level 1	Tag Line (Value Proposition)		
Level 2	Topic 1	Topic 2	Topic 3
Level 3	Value 1	Value 1	Value 1
	Value 2	Value 2	Value 2
	Value 3	Value 3	Value 3
Level 4	Story 1	Story 1	Story 1
	Story 2	Story 2	Story 2
	Story 3	Story 3	Story 3
Level 5	Detail 1	Detail 1	Detail 1
	Detail 2	Detail 2	Detail 2
	Detail 3	Detail 3	Detail 3

Structured Conversation

So how do you write out your story? This is simple. If you look back at your resume, pick out the "Wow!" accomplishments that illustrate each value. Take the first one and write a brief (short) two- to three-minute story of what you did. Next you practice delivering your story into a recorder and then play it back. You will be amazed how often this leads you to change the story so that it says what you really want to say. That is a good thing.

Try writing out your story in a simple sentence structure.

But wait! How can I tell my "story" in only two or three minutes? I need twenty minutes!

If you cannot get it down to two or three minutes, you will lose your audience, lose your credibility as an executive, and damage your brand. That is not a good thing.

Remember the concept of layering? You want a dialogue (read: conversation). You tell your brief story and watch for nonverbals or questions. If no questions come, I recommend you go back up a level to talk about your Value #2 in the chart above and repeat the process in a conversational and friendly dialogue tone. Or it may be time to move on to the next person.

Here is the key: If you spill your guts, your audience will get more than they want – and have no follow-up questions. If you leave them hanging with a good story, they will want more – either now or by getting together later. Aha! That is your goal. Get the interest in a follow-up meeting where you have more time to talk.

Your goal should be no more than ten minutes with anyone at a networking meeting unless they are a major decision maker or influencer and *they* ask for more. They rarely will want more (they need to network themselves), but they may be open to getting breakfast or coffee on another day. Mission accomplished.

Why list "detail" (level 5) in the previous chart? In the rare case that your audience is totally absorbed in your story, you need to be able to provide the next level of detail of how you accomplished your story. Better yet, be prepared to share *brief* details that back up your story.

If you have done your homework or asked great questions before talking, you can often apply your value, story, and detail in such a way that the listener can relate to it in his own business.

Make sure you are comfortable with your stories. Ask your teenager to listen and provide feedback. You might be amazed at the questions they will ask which help you to be clearer to a CEO-level audience. That is, in everyday English, not jargon. You may also find your relationship with your teenager improving by talking to them and truly listening to their input.

Want to learn more? For more information on how to use your own stories, try *Whoever Tells the Best Story Wins* by Annette Simmons.

Chapter Six

Step Five: Developing Your Marketing Plan

Review What You Have

M ost people fail to plan, which often results in their "planning to fail."

By now you are probably tired. I recommend you take a break and be sure the prior steps are where you want them. You need to be fresh to start this process.

First, begin collecting data. Here are some questions to ask and data to collect:

- ➢ How much time do you have before you risk losing your house? A job may be better than the best job. A temporary assignment can help provide funding and keep your skills current. A number of "rent an executive" firms exist.
- ➢ What is your personal financial picture? Do you have money that you can budget for your search? If so, how much and over what time frame?
- ➢ Who do you know? Make an exhaustive list.
  - ▪ Employed executive friends

- Employed influencer friends
- Clients
- Vendors
- Consultants and subcontractors
- Influential firms (legal, accounting, banking, etc.)
- In transition friends
- In transition influencer friends
- Pastor, priest, rabbi
- Church or synagogue friends
- Neighbors
- Parents of your children's friends, sports activities, or community organizations, i.e. Boy Scouts, soccer, football, tennis...
- Prayer groups, Bible studies, clubs, and association contacts...
- Relatives
- Anyone else you can think of or whom your spouse can think of
    You never know which contact will bring the friend of a friend who has the perfect job!

➤ Make a list of all networking groups and events that are in town. Do not leave any out! Examples in Atlanta include:
- FENG (Financial Executive Networking Group)
- Kettering (C-Level executives)
- SENG (Strategic Executive Networking Group)
- TENG (Technology Executive Networking Group)
- The Ritz Group
- ACG (Association for Corporate Growth)
- Roswell United Methodist Church (almost any major church will have a program)
- Christian-sponsored transition help groups, such as Crossroads Career Network
- Women in Business

- Technology executive groups
- CFO Roundtables
- CEO Groups (such as Vistage or FCCI)
- Law firm presentations
- University presentations
- Association meetings
- Chamber of Commerce meetings
- Clubs (Rotary, Key Club, Lions, Kiwanis, Knights of Columbus, etc.)
- School alumni clubs (Harvard Club, Ivy League Club, Georgia Tech Club, etc.)
- Catalyst breakfast meetings
- *Business Chronicle* sponsored meetings
- Christian or Jewish sponsored events
- Country club events
- You get the picture. Ask around.

➢ Make a list of all retained recruiters. Lists are available in excellent books such as *Rites of Passage* by John Lucht. Highlight those whom you know. Ask peers whom they know and like.

➢ Make a list of funding groups (VC, Angels, etc.)

➢ Make a list of those companies in your town that may fit your passion and need your services. You can always expand outside of your town as needed.

➢ Make a list of social networks (on the Internet) that can help. Popular networks include LinkedIn, Plaxo, Pulse, ZoomInfo, Spoke, and many others.

That is enough to get started. I recommend you begin the list and then continue to step six while continuing to ask others for advice and contacts.

Note Well: If you need money *now*, consider working for temporary (rent a body) groups. Executive-level groups are around and growing. You may also choose to work for such a group to get specific experience that you currently lack but need to qualify for the job of your dreams. It is not unusual to land at a company where you are doing contract work.

Now go back through the list and prioritize who is best positioned to help and which networking events may have the type of decision makers or influencers you need to get to know.

If you have steps one through five completed, you are almost ready to talk to them, but not yet.

Now develop a metric to chart what you plan to do each day or week. For example, I need to call ten friends, attend two networking events, go to five follow-up breakfast or lunch meetings, make twenty cold calls, go play golf (oops, how did that get in here?), have two telephone interviews, write ten personal notes and thank-you notes, and... You decide what your goals are.

A friend of mine, John Hughes, developed a chart that might be helpful. I modified it slightly for a broader audience:

Activity	Mon	Tues	Weds	Thurs	Fri	Sat	Sun
Interviews							
HR screens							
In-person networking with executives							
Telephone networking with executives							
Meet with other network group members							

Networking meetings

Job leads shared

Notes and comments:

> **Note Well:** The list does not include resumes sent, Web job search responses, or head hunters talked to. You can add those, but this marketing plan focuses on networking, which represents 80 percent of how executives get back in the saddle. Networking is also the process few include in their marketing plan.

John Hughes also points out that it is important to note the chart is hierarchical–you engage in activities at the lower end (i.e. attending networking meetings) with the intention of using those events to get to the next level of the hierarchy (i.e. setting up one-on-one meetings with network group members from the networking meeting). You repeat this process until it culminates eventually in interviews. Since this "climb up the hierarchy" takes time and you should be pursuing multiple opportunities simultaneously, each week you will have activities at various levels of the hierarchy.

As you call friends or meet people in network events, your goal is to get two referral introductions from everyone. That way, your list of people to talk to will expand. Be sure not to violate your brand image.

Chapter Seven

Step Six: Getting Your Message Out

✐

Networking, Networking, Networking...Is the Secret to Success

S ince 80 percent of jobs come through networking, why don't more executives pursue it?

I believe it is because of one or more of the following excuses:

1. I was never taught. (That excuse is about to go away)
2. I was never mentored. (Did you ever ask?)
3. I am not a sales person. (Most salespeople don't network much either)
4. I don't have time. (Time is an investment. Is having a job a good return?)
5. I do not understand the rules of the game. (Most attendees don't either)

Let's first dive into general principles. Then we will walk through an example.

Networking Principle #1: Big cities are really small town networks

I live in Atlanta. It is really a large city comprised of many smaller cities. Each smaller city has a social, business, political, and expertise informal pecking order. For example, there is the opera crowd, the non-profit crowd, the service club crowd, the executive's transition crowd, the M&A/VC crowd, Christian or Jewish groups/studies, the school affiliation crowd, the university presentation crowd, various associations' crowds, the small business crowd, local city politics and events, etc. You get the idea. Once you examine these groups, you will be amazed how many there are!

You will also find that these groups have local pecking orders and are often informally tied to the "big boy" pecking order. That means you can be recognized as important and influential in a suburb city group and not recognized at all as an Atlanta key player or influencer.

The reverse is different. If you are an Atlanta-wide key player or influencer, it is highly likely that the smaller groups will recognize you and look up to you. Your "brand" will precede you.

This is important. That means your reputation, accomplishments, dress, style, and all elements of your brand will proceed positively or negatively. It also means that one enemy can damage you. On the other hand, the "right" people liking you can propel you to new heights and new warm connections.

As an example, if you are trying to raise capital in the venture capital community but the first VC group does not like your solution, company plan, or you, then it is highly likely that all the other VC groups will hear about it and shy away from wanting to even talk to you.

What is going on? It is all about trust. Most of us have been harmed by someone who said one thing but did something else or did not perform as promised. So we naturally are cautious about everyone. If one of the trusted "connected" tells his friends you are worth talking to, that is a green flag. If they raise a yellow or red flag, you might as well go elsewhere. Your brand becomes the commodity that is either accepted or rejected.

That is why the passion/vision/branding/value process is so important. You cannot afford to create the wrong first impression with a "connected" player. Since you do not know who those "connected players" are, I recommend you treat everyone as if they are "connected." Even if someone is not "connected" you never know who they know and whether or not they are "influencers." The key is to constantly communicate your brand.

Networking Principle #2: It is not who you know, it is who knows you

I "know" many people in Atlanta, Philadelphia, Dallas, and other places where I lived or traveled. The real question is how many players or influencers in those cities know me?

Let's use a classic large company as an example. You can argue that this does not apply to you, but humor me.

I used to run a global organization in a large multinational company. When I would fly into a regional office, I would know very few people but be introduced around as a "big man." Actually, I did have more weight then. They would come up to me and use my name and I could not remember most of them, even when I returned the next time. Who would I remember? Those who were at a similar level or higher and those who directly reported to me. Have you ever experienced a similar situation?

The test when you go to a networking meeting is when people come up to you, use your first name, and start talking to you as if they know you, when you don't have a clue who they are. Either you just forgot who they are (not good) or they see you as an influencer or player who might help them (good).

I strongly recommend you do not ignore the "little people" for a host of reasons we will discuss later, but when you have players or influencers coming up to you and using your name, then you can say they know you. Now you know you are making progress.

<u>Networking Principle #3: Seek lifelong friends, not a job</u>

Here is a major secret to networking. If you go with the attitude of meeting and finding new friends whom *you* can help, then you will find networking to be fun and rewarding, and you will come across as a peer player and influencer. If you go to find a job, land funding, or procure some other single-shot objective, then you will come across as a user and abuser of people. That is not the brand you can afford. It will keep you out of being accepted by those who only deal with people they trust.

So where do you start? First, find the networking group that fits your goals. Second, start with the "little people." Why?

1. You need the practice
2. Little people often grow up to be big people
3. Big people watch how you treat little people
4. Little people have friends and mentors
5. You never really know who is a "little person," a player, or an influencer
6. The more people you help, the higher your brand value
7. You can help "little people." You need "big people" to help you.

At the end of the day, we are all in this together and need each other. Lend a hand. Some groups call this "paying it forward." That means you help someone whether they can help you or not, while believing that someone at sometime will pay it back with interest. You just don't know who or when.

In my case, I do not network for personal advantage. I enjoy helping people. It is a lifestyle. Do I occasionally benefit from a referral or introduction? Of course I do. I always appreciate them, but I will not cheapen my brand by insisting on a payback.

You make friends through networking. When you need help, you will find friends ready to help.

If you are new to networking, now is the time to start. If you have a sincere interest in making friends, it will show and many will be willing to help you in return by helping you get back into the saddle. They, like me, want to help people. Just don't abuse them. Be appreciative. Help others. Develop a lifestyle of making new friends.

Networking Principle #4: Help others help you

Heard this before? I will keep repeating it because it is the *greatest secret* to networking.

If you cannot help others help you, then how can they help you?

You can be a jerk but know how to present yourself in a way others can see how to help you. Or you can be a great guy trying to help others who is not clear, does not know how to ask for help, and is confused about who he is and what he needs!

Assume most people in a networking group are willing to listen and help. Assume that you will find jerks who only care about their interests, so move on. In both cases, the primary purpose of networking is to get brand recognition.

This takes us back to your passion/vision/value proposition/brand. What is your brand? How do you bring value? What are you looking for? How can I help you?

At a minimum, you want them to remember you and your tagline – period. If you do not succeed here, you most likely will not get to the next steps.

So how do you help others help you? Here is a suggestion. How you personalize it is up to you and the situation.

Step One: Share your name, listen for ways of helping others, ask questions about them. Seek to be a friend.

If nothing else happens, you did not create a bad impression.

You will be amazed at what people say when you engage in personal dialogue. You will learn what interests them, what you may have in common, who you may know in common, and what issues or concerns they have.

Now you are accomplishing several objectives: learning how you might be able to help them, learning what things you have in mutual (trust is often based on common beliefs and experiences), and becoming someone he is more likely to remember than all the other glad-handers.

Notice that in this case you may not have even been asked about your brand or who you are. But they will probably remember you. A great start.

Even better, if you notice that the person you are talking to can be helped by introducing them to someone else in the crowd, introduce them. That provides immediate assistance. People notice. Also, that is what a friend would do.

Step Two: First impressions count—don't waste them.

If you are dressed right, smiling, relaxed, and enjoying helping others, the first impression is usually good.

Don't spoil it by opening your mouth unless you are ready.

When they ask about you (99 percent certainty unless they are self-absorbed), keep it brief. Do not vomit your entire history on them.

Remember, your goals are:

1. Good first impression
2. A clear concise brand—that is what they will remember about you
3. Maybe some short discussion about your brand and value
4. Maybe some short discussion about how they may be able to help you
5. Hopefully, agreement to meet privately for coffee, breakfast, or lunch when you have more time and focus to talk at a deeper level
6. Leave them wanting to know more, looking forward to meeting you later
7. Let them move on to the next person. This elevates your brand and communicates that you understand they are there to network themselves, not to be cornered.

So now we assume you are ready to talk about yourself. Have your well-rehearsed brand and value statement to explain who you are. You have five to ten seconds for the first sentence. You have a maximum of thirty seconds to include your value proposition. Now STOP! You want their reaction. If non-interest is apparent, plan to move on. If nonverbal interest or a question to you results, you have the green light to share another statement or example.

The key is dialogue that is interesting but not so complete that there is no reason to meet later to talk more.

Feel free to use your short stories and tree diagram to answer questions.

Hope that the conversation moves off of you and onto a problem they share or a problem a friend of theirs has which you might be able to be the solution for or know someone else who might be the solution.

Remember, friends help other friends solve problems. If you are the solution, there is mutual benefit to talk more. If you are not the solution but are willing to help point them in the right direction, they are usually appreciative and will ask how they can help you. Either way, everyone wins.

Key concept: If I win and you lose (I use you), I will lose in the long run. Try for a win-win-win!

Getting a meeting of mutual interest or an introduction to someone else is a bonus, if you are interesting.

Step Three: Write down what you found out and your meeting objectives

When the person leaves, write down notes on their business card to remind you of action items or points of interest. Otherwise, you will find a pocketful of cards and forget which one was the one you wanted to remember or, worse, forget the action item.

When you get in the car or get home, go through all your cards and organize them.

For those who mean nothing, put them in a pile in case you need to look another day. Keep a historical stack. I use an index card box. You never know when someone you thought was not helpful turns out to be a key contact.

For those who were players or influencers but not action items, note them and keep their information handy.

For those who had action items, make a To Do list and be sure it gets done.

For those who agreed to a meeting, call or email to set up the meeting. Then create a file to write down what you remember from the conversation, what your meeting objectives are, and how you might be able to help them. Be sure to call or email to confirm the day before. Be sure to be early to the meeting. Have their cell number in case they are late or lost. Call after fifteen or twenty minutes if they are late.

Follow up the meeting with a handwritten thank-you note (a class act).

Want to learn more? Other resources that my friend Martin Schmidler suggests include www. relationshipeconomics.net and the books *Selling to VITO, the Very Important Top Officer* and *Getting to VITO* by Anthony Parinello, and *People Styles at Work* by Robert Bolton.

Chapter Eight

Step Seven: Creating Your Marketing Document

Notice I did not say resume! You should carry your resume to the meeting but only use it if strongly requested. Instead, you need to focus on talking face to face and eyeball to eyeball.

Have you ever been to a meeting where the speaker is using PowerPoint? Each chart has fifty words. You soon fall asleep (mentally, not literally) and start thinking about other things. Consider your resume as having the same result. Remember, our audience is mostly Type A executives.

Have you ever been to a meeting where the speaker was passionate, used no notes, did not use PowerPoint props, and was speaking to you and asking you questions? Did you ever fall asleep in that meeting?

That is why we focus on a one-page marketing document. A marketing document is a tool to *help others help you*. It is a brochure. It is a leave-behind. It has everything the person you are meeting with needs to know at this stage – and *how he can help you*.

What stage is that? It is the follow-up meeting that was agreed to during the networking meeting or a referral meeting.

We will discuss the meeting in chapter nine. Let's talk about what a marketing document looks like.

Allow me to give credit to whichever outplacement firm came up with the general idea. The following is my modification of that document.

First, it is one page in size with 12-point font. Not two pages. Not size 8 font.

Second, it has three main sections. Each section should take one-third of the page.

The first section is your name, contact information, and value proposition. The value proposition is a one- to two-sentence summary of how your brand can help them solve a problem. That is all! Keep white space. If they later look at one thing, this should be what they remember and what they use to refer you to a friend. The reaction you want is, "You're the man who ...." For me, I want to be known as the expense management guy or the identity theft solutions guy. Everything else is detail.

The second section begins with a brief statement of what your objective is followed by an executive summary. This is to include a short bullet point outline of up to three points that support your value proposition followed by the areas of expertise you wish to highlight. The purpose is to document what you said earlier in the meeting.

Let's take a look at an example:

Joe Smith, CPA
123 Perimeter Park Drive
Atlanta, GA 30341
678-444-1111 cell
Joe.Smith@host.com

Value Proposition:
CFO with repeated success in company growth and liquidity events.

Search Objective:
Chief Financial Officer for private equity funded high-growth technology play

Executive Summary:
CPA with private equity and turnaround experience in software and Internet technology companies. Business partner in running finance, acquisitions, and operational growth for $26 million, $50 million, and $72 million liquidity events, respectively.

Areas of Expertise Include:

- Strategic Planning
- Acquisitions, Due Diligence; Mergers and Consolidations
- Board & Investor Communications
- Banking and Funding Management
- Financial Operations
- Internal Controls - Development and Implementation
- Right-sizing of Operations, People Management, Motivation, and Development
- Systems Implementation

Characteristics of Target Company:

Size: 50 or more employees
Sales: $20 to $100+ million
Structure: Private company or company owned by
             private equity group

Networking Venues: ACG, FENG, Kettering, and medium-size legal, accounting, and banking firms.

Companies of Interest:

Software Companies	Internet Companies
- ABC Corporation	- Investment Systems
- EFG Company	- Hot Games, Inc.
- Exciting Group	- China View Company
- HIJ Software	- Global Healthcare Solutions
- LMN Development	- Recruiter's World
- OPQ Resources	- RST Systems

Notice a few points.

1. There is a lot of white space. Keep it simple. Leave room for notes.
2. The value proposition is short but communicates why someone should want to talk to you or refer you.
3. The search objective is short and ties into the value proposition.
4. The executive summary is short but adds one to three points that provide back-up proof of your success in adding value.
5. The listing of stories is left off. You can add three topics, but I recommend you squeeze into the exec-

utive summary at such a high level they beg to be asked about by the reader. In the illustration above, the logical question is "tell me about these three liquidity events..." Do not try to answer every question. You want brand presence without getting tactical. Otherwise, you lower your brand value.

6. The areas of expertise are those required to tie into your value proposition. Notice the use of "financial operations" to describe all the types you could list separately (accounting, FP&A, treasury, cash, inventory...) and the use of "systems implementation" is used to cover the bases. They can always ask what type of system but usually will not bother at the CEO level. Don't clutter with details that you can speak to if asked.

The third section is designed to trigger discussion and assistance for referrals and introductions. First, what size and type of company are you looking for? You must limit your scope. If too broad, the reader cannot focus and will usually give up.

Note.   The purpose of the marketing document is to help them help you.

After the target company characteristics, I added networking venues. They may have ideas you have not considered. If the networking event is members-only or invitees-only, they may be willing to bring you along as a guest or invitee. DO NOT MISS THIS OPPORTUNITY.

Third, is the list of targeted companies you have researched, attempted to find someone to refer you, and fit your value proposition.

The list of targeted companies is usually neglected. It is hard work. It means you have been seriously looking and know some of each company's players and issues.

Note Well: **The purpose of the targeted compa nies is to a) focus the reader to talk about any listed company to help you get in at the right level through a personal referral and b) stimulate the thinking of the reader for the names of non-listed companies which fit a similar profile.**

I recommend that you do not hand out the marketing document at the beginning of the meeting. You want a two-way conversation that allows the dialogue to flow in any direction that the person you are meeting with wishes to go. Remember, you are on his time – but you do want to be sure to verbally review the value proposition, search objective, and executive summary. If you are careful, you can usually direct the conversation to characteristics of target companies and networking venues.

Notice that areas of expertise are skipped unless needed. Most CEOs, unless they are interested in hiring, do not need this level of detail at this time. However, listing it as part of your leave-behind brochure is a good idea.

If all goes well, feel free to bring out the marketing document to then focus on companies of interest. Remember, the point of the meeting is to get referrals. The list helps the person you are meeting with to focus and stimulate his thoughts to see if he knows anyone in the listed companies or to think of someone who should be on your list that you should meet. If he is willing to introduce you, congratulations!

Now, by leaving the marketing document behind, you are giving the person the statements he can use to introduce you. You have done most of the work. You have helped him to help you!

Even if you do not hand out the marketing document, you will benefit by going through the process of creating it. As you gain experience in the networking or referral meeting, you will sense when to pull it out or keep it in your pocket. As in all meetings, the key is a good impression, a simple and memorable tagline, and good mutual dialogue. A marketing document is only a tool to reinforce those objectives and to leave behind as a reminder of who you are.

Chapter Nine

Step Eight: Meeting the Friend's Friend

When a neighbor, former work associate, or networking contact wants to meet with you or refer you to one of their friends, there is a lot at risk. There is also a lot that can be gained.

Make a Good Impression

First, if you do a credible job, your brand recognition grows and opens the door for others to be willing to refer you. Second, the person you are meeting with may have a job opening, may create a job for you, may refer you, or you may never hear from them again. Therefore, your first objective is to make a friend and come across as a valuable solution to someone's problem. Fail to do this and your brand turns negative at one hundred times the rate.

I cannot overemphasize the importance of making a good impression. That means being appropriately dressed, groomed, well-mannered, friendly, relaxed, confident, knowledgeable, and competent. If not, three things happen:

1. Word gets around that you are merely a wannabe. No senior executive has time for a wannabe unless the executive agrees ahead that the meeting purpose is to help a junior person. That means, even if you are a current CFO or CEO, you will suffer damage to your image and brand.
2. No serious consideration of a job or referring to hiring managers will be made.
3. If someone else referred you, their brand (credibility) is also on the line. Honor the referee. Both brands are at stake. So is the referee's trust in you.

Be Prepared for the Meeting

Preparing for these meetings is critical. You do not have to spend as much time as with an interviewing company, but a review of their website and understanding issues they face is useful.

Top executives are willing to brainstorm and help each other. You need to understand something about them to prepare you for the meeting. You need to understand something about their company, because that is where they live.

You are not there to solve their problems unless it turns into a job interview. You are trying to discover as much common ground as possible to "connect" on a personal basis.

Friends help friends. Friends trust friends. Not being prepared means you do not care enough to want to get to know them. It communicates that you merely wish to use them for your own benefit. Ouch.

Try to Help Them

If you try to help the other person, they will be more likely to be willing to help you.

Often you will not see an immediate payback. Networking organizations call this "paying it forward." The idea is that someone at sometime will pay you back in multiples.

Besides, life is much more enjoyable if you help others.

It also is a guarantee to help continue building your brand and others trust in you.

Watch for Signs and React Appropriately

Be sensitive to the time allowed. DO NOT EXCEED the time agreed upon unless both parties indicate verbally that more time is warranted.

Look for nonverbal signals. If the other party is uncomfortable, busy, distracted, or avoiding meaningful conversation, it may suggest rescheduling is warranted or it may suggest that you ran into a dead end and should move on. Remember, your brand is at stake. If the other person is relaxed and engaged, keep looking for signs that it is time to wrap up. This actually helps keep you from "spilling out far too much information." If he asks a question the size of a thimble of water, don't give him a shower. When in doubt, keep it short and see if he wants more. It is always better to leave while he wants more.

Not Every Opportunity Fits You

Networking is a numbers game. Most people you meet will not be able to help you. Some people can hurt you. A few will be beneficial. You never know when you start which is which. As many mothers tell their daughters, you may have to kiss a lot of frogs to find your prince.

That is life. That is sales. That is the game in networking. You only need one homerun to make it all worthwhile. Be patient and not anxious. It will show.

If you were referred by someone else, send them a thank-you note and a brief status of the meeting's results. Try to be positive. You never know what may happen. If you are negative, nothing good will happen. Try to find something good to report, even if it is that you had a great opportunity to practice meeting other people.

Chapter Ten

Step Nine: Working on Your Power Resume

Why Not Work on Your Resume Earlier?

You could write your resume earlier, but until you go through the previous process I believe you would be wasting your time. Until you have written down your value proposition and your key stories, you are not really ready to create a resume that works. Until you practice your value proposition and key stories in a networking environment, you will not have the chance to hone your message.

First impressions are critical. Job interviews are often a first-impression and one-shot opportunity. If you were referred into the job interview, you are representing yourself and the one who made the referral. Make it count.

Why now? Now you need your resume for a job referral or interview. What is the difference? Through networking you may be referred to someone who has a job lead or a job opening. Or a recruiter or company may call you about a specific job. Now you must be sure your resume is ready for the big time. If you get the job lead earlier in the process, you do the best you can.

At this stage, even if the hiring manager wants to hire you, you still have human resources to go through. You have to have a resume.

What Is a Power Resume?

First, it is not a mere history of your job experience. It is a marketing tool that includes far more detail than your marketing document. Your marketing document is designed to help in the networking process for others to help you. Your resume is the tool that helps the hiring manager feel comfortable that everything others told him about you and that what you told him is backed up by another layer of proof. The resume also helps HR certify that you are "qualified."

That means the focus is primarily on your future, not your past. The resume must restate your value proposition, include your key stories, and provide quantified evidence that back up your stories. Of course, it must also include a job history that shows your progression building up to your last job and shows why you are now qualified to take the next logical step toward your future dream job.

A power resume accomplishes this mission two ways.

First, a generic power resume is important to have with you at all times. You never know when you may need it. Try not to pass it around unless you need to do so. A true high-level executive diminishes his brand by throwing his paper around on the street. Second, a job interview power resume has slight changes designed specifically for the company where you are interviewing. We will cover this topic later under interviewing.

Make Ten Pages into Two Pages

The first hurdle you face is to understand that no matter who tells you otherwise, *no resume should ever exceed two pages.*

The challenge that most of us Type A personalities have is that our accomplishments are so many, we could write ten pages. Go ahead. Ten pages will give you a deep well from which to selectively pick what is best for your value proposition and the specific company where you are interviewing.

There Is No One Best Model

Everyone has their opinion on how a resume should look. Books and consultants abound to help you adopt *their template.* I am not going to recommend one design. Different fields, different levels, different industries, and different audiences result in there being many different cultures and viewpoints.

The best solution is to design the best resume you can and pass it around to others for their comments. Have your recruiter friends, peers, HR friends, and marketing communication friends look at your resume from their perspective. If it is clear, forward-focused, backs up the job you are seeking, and shows HR evidence that you can substantiate your story, then you have your generic power resume ready to enter the game.

So what does a power resume look like? There is no one answer. I pulled up ten different resumes from my files and found ten different styles and formats. I decided to create one based upon an actual resume of a friend. I changed the names but used much of his content.

The following resume is for a sales executive. You should be able to adapt it to your background and level. You can also see how it differs from a marketing document, yet builds upon it.

Joe D. Smith

123 Perimeter Park Drive	Home Phone: 678-444-1111
Atlanta, GA	E-mail: joe.smith@host.com

Chief Sales Executive with 20 years of exceptional sales and marketing leadership in national and regional organizations selling to medium to large corporate environments.

KEY QUALIFICATIONS:

Strategic Sales Team Development	P&L Performance
Complex Product and Services Sales	Strategic Planning
Customer Retention and	Marketing
Expansion	Program
	Development

PROFESSIONAL EXPERIENCE:

Fortune 100 Corporation, Inc. - Atlanta, GA 2001-2007
Vice President, ABC Divisional Sales 2004-2007
ABC Division is the outsourcing services division for Fortune 100 Corporation, Inc. Services include software solutions, business process consulting, systems integration, business support services, and onsite facilities management services.

- Grew revenue by 28% in three years
- Turned around ($3.6M) profit to $8.0M
- Grew annual contracts by 342%
- Raised customer retention rate to 93%
- Re-engineered sales and marketing to support new vision

- Managed 7 regional sales managers and 46 account managers

*Director Strategic Marketing, EFG Subsidiary*2001-2004
- Created innovative tool to align strategic initiatives with CRM technologies
  - Quadrant view of financial results and non-financial metrics by channel
  - Report card for business unit adoption of strategic initiatives
- Improved ROI for incentive programs while staying within budget
- Managed organization of 24 responsible for Channel Planning, MarCom, Public Relations, Incentives & Promotions, Business Analysis, and Competitive Analysis

Incredible Business Solutions – Atlanta, GA1999-2001
Partner
Incredible Business Solutions is a national recruiting firm in sales, sales management, and executive placements in the technology and services industries. Incredible Business Solutions was purchased by Hire USA of Atlanta, GA.
- Recruited executives, sales managers, and sales reps
- Created business plans, performance metrics, sales process, and activity standards

Fortune 500 Corporation, Inc. – Atlanta, GA1987-1999
Fortune 500 Corporation, Inc., solutions include products, software, and applications for document management.

National Director of Sales   1997-1999
- Increased sales by 15% per year
- Created compensation plans, performance metrics, activity standards, training programs, and incentive programs

- Managed 8 regional sales managers and 55 account managers

Marketing Director, Digital and High Volume Products
– Atlanta, GA 1995-1997
Marketing Manager, High Volume Products
– Atlanta, GA 1993-1995
District Manager – Detroit, MI 1991-1993
District Manager – Toledo, OH 1990-1991
Commercial Sales Manager – Detroit, MI 1989-1990
Regional Manpower Development Manager
– Chicago, IL 1988-1989
Territory Sales Rep – Chicago, IL 1987-1988

EDUCATION:
University of Chicago
B.A. in Communications

PROFESSIONAL TRAINING
- Advanced Leadership Workshop — Falcon Performance Strategic Selling
- Leadership Effectiveness Workshop — Strategic Account Selling
- Ken Blanchard Situational Leadership — Miller Heiman Strategic Selling
- Management Essentials I & II — Customer Vision Training 1-8
- DISC/Predictive Index/ Wonderlic Training — Principles and Ethics Training

AWARDS AND DISTINCTIONS:
- "Top 100" Award Trip in 2006
- Champion of Corporate Customer Vision Team 2002-2004

- Main stage presenter at National Managers Conference for 12 years
- Numerous sales and management performance awards 1988-1993
- Support for Junior Achievement at Carey Reynolds School 2002-2007

Note the structure:

- Significant white space. Interviewers can write notes based on conversation
- Not too much detail. Just enough to show results, scope, and progression
- Progression supports value proposition, which was stated at the top
- Key qualifications related to the stories supporting the value proposition; details support the stories
- Basic format is familiar to most executives and HR. Does not distract and is easy to follow
- Does not try to answer every question – just the questions most hiring managers would ask. You want them to ask on a specific point so you can verbally dialogue with your story, illustration, or example.
- The goal of a resume is not the interview. The interview is a mutual selling situation containing mutual questions, dialogue, nonverbal observations, and testing of the "likeability" factor. The goal of the resume is to provide structure to back-up claims and for HR to nod their heads in agreement of your qualifications.

No matter what your resume looks like, if you follow these guidelines, you can distinguish yourself from others who write too much, are not clear, use jargon, or use flowery descriptions. Keep to the point. Keep it short. Have a complete overview designed to encourage dialogue.

Chapter Eleven

Step Ten: Preparing for Your Interview

S ince there are numerous books on how to prepare for an interview, I will not bore you with details but will build upon others.

Interviews Are a Two-Way Street

If you learn nothing else from this book, note that the interview is *a two-way street.*

Most job applicants go into the interview ready to put their best foot forward to sell why they should get the job. Nothing wrong with that – except they forget the second half of the interview! If the company is hiring a high-level executive, don't you think the company will try to put its best foot forward?

How long does a company take to search for the right executive candidate? How much does a recruiter charge to find the right candidate? How much is at stake if the company hires the wrong candidate?

Now put the shoe on your foot. You have momentum. You have built up your network. You are a star waiting for the right opportunity to spread your wings and make a significant impact to the company. To do so you will leave your networking activities and perhaps even move. The risk you are taking is huge. What if you take the job and later find out that it was a mistake? How much will that cost you? How much will it cost your family? What will you do then?

To be frank, I have taken two jobs where the hiring teams lied to me. Okay, they may have only misrepresented or spun the facts. I was fooled but I did learn some expensive lessons. So have many of my executive friends. Please do not repeat our mistakes.

The interview is for you to find out more about the company than is publicly available. You need to see if they are telling the truth, if their culture fits you, and if they will let you do what you know you need to do. If you sense a "no" to any of those criteria, I recommend you thank them for their time and leave.

Use the interview as a two-way conversation.

Use Questions to Direct Conversation and Engagement

You are used to being peppered with their standard questions. You are ready to answer their trick questions and can even read between the lines. How many questions do you have? They should be open-ended and engaging. The trick is to ask an outstanding question and then be silent for a minute. You will be amazed at what you might learn.

Keep in mind that the people you are interviewing with today are also the ones you might be working with tomorrow. You want to establish a working relationship with them. You might also wish to engage them as a potential friend. At a minimum, you will stand out from other interviews and establish an emotional tie that others might have missed.

Most decisions are based on gut instinct (emotions) rather than facts. Ask good business questions (not personal questions) that show you have learned about the company and have a sincere interest in wanting to know more about the people and working environment.

Use Questions to Find Out "Hidden" Points

Ever talk to an interviewer who does not like to talk about their company? If so, either they are rare or they do not like their company. Let them open up to you. You might find that you should "run" or you might find that their pain is something you can eliminate if you get the job.

Try to Make Friends with Everyone – Run From Unfriendly Cultures

You will usually spend more time at the office than with your family. For many, you may spend over ten hours a day with work associates and less than one hour talking to your children or spouse. Liking the people, the culture, and the environment is critical to your being able to focus on enjoying the challenges of growing the company.

Try to make friends with everyone. If the first person is not friendly, that may not mean anything. If most of the people are not friendly, there may be a reason. Try to find out why. Run from unfriendly cultures. The last thing you need is to be unhappy at work and then come home miserable to your sweet, loving, waiting family. Life is too short.

How to Find the Questions to Ask

Whenever I talk to confident and successful executives about how they prepared for their interview, they usually all have the same response. They prepared for days to know a͡s much about the company as possible, to know what th҃ issues were, to script questions to ask, and to scri͉ answer questions the company may not ask but should have asked. Usually you will surprise them with your knowledge. Their impression of you could change from hiring for a job at the lowest total cost to landing you at whatever cost it takes!

So how do you find the questions to ask?

First, look up every reference possible on the Internet. Read the company website. Read all publicly disclosed information and reports. Read stock analyst analyses. Read the blogs and bulletin boards. Draft critical questions that come to your mind. Find areas of pain that you can help solve. Script questions around those pains for which you already have a prepared answer in your hip pocket.

Do not try to tell them *how* to solve their problems. Great questions and comments to their responses will confirm that you may be the one to solve them.

Second, network through others to find current employees or recent employees who might be able to give firsthand insight into the company. Be sure to ask them questions on culture, honesty, treatment, issues, and personalities. You would be amazed at the insights you might receive. Just don't tell the interviewer that you talked to those people. The interviewer might think you walk on water!

So where do you find these employees? The first place is through your network or the network of a friend who knows a friend…. The second place is through your association. For example, I can search the 26,000-member national database on financial executives who may have worked there before or still work there now. I could also search the 1,200-member local executive database where I am a member.

If you use Plaxo or LinkedIn, you can often find someone who is connected to someone who can help. These tools can be highly useful or abused. Just be careful who you include within your network.

A more risky approach is to use Internet social networking sites such as Facebook. Just remember that you might find the right or wrong person. You definitely need to be careful about saying something online that will stay on the Internet past your lifetime.

Another excellent source is those who are trusted advisers to the company. If you know the accounting audit firm, legal counsel, bankers, and others who may have invaluable insights and the willingness to share them, make that opportunity count. As a high-level executive, they will be interested in your potential success and in seeing you bring success to their client. They should not share anything that violates a trust.

The more people you can talk to before the interview, the more prepared you will be and the better the questions will be for you to decide if you really do like the company and for them to see how proactive you are in pursuing the job opportunity. The assumption is that you would use the same methodology as a key to success in the new job.

Get the Offer

Your goal is to always get an offer. You can always turn it down if you have concerns about the company or if you have other companies that you are mutually interested in pursuing. You cannot accept an offer that you do not get!

Want to learn more? Read the book *Neuromarketing* by Patrick Renvoise and Christophe Morin, Thomas Nelson, 2007. You need to understand their concepts before going into an interview situation.

Suggestions from friends include: *Topgrading: How Leading Companies Win by Hiring, Coaching, and Keeping the Best People* by Bradford D. Smart and *Knock 'Em Dead 2006* by Martin Yate.

Chapter Twelve

Step Eleven: Negotiating Your Terms

The best news is a call with a job offer and a discussion of what terms would be acceptable to you. Some rules of thumb are:

Be Ready for the Question About Your Requirements

You should have already done your homework. If not, I recommend you start now.

First, you need to know your market value. What do people with your experience and talents typically earn in this industry for this level? What limits of vacation, relocation, benefits, and perks are typical for your level and experience? What are you willing to give up in order to negotiate more elsewhere?

The first place to look is on the Internet at job postings, friendly retained recruiters (not the one helping you get placed), and Internet studies. The second place is through friends and based upon your experience. The third area to look is in public financial statements of the company that may be hiring you. You can often see the entire compensation and contract of your potential boss! Good guess that you will not exceed that package, but you may be able to get similar terms.

The final place to look is to get professional help. No, I do not mean a psychiatrist. I mean from labor lawyers or professional labor negotiators. In some negotiations, companies understand your need for representation and will provide a reasonable amount to fund it as part of the job offer.

Be careful not to target too high unless you are willing to walk away.

Negotiating a Contract

At the executive level, you need help. I strongly recommend legal representation. State and federal laws constantly change. State laws vary. Best practices and norms also change. What was true the last time you negotiated may not be true today.

One example is termination due to a merger or acquisition. Many friends of mine have made significant gains due to golden handcuffs or options maturing upon the sale of their company. This area should be high on your wish list, particularly if the company is a high-growth opportunity. You need tightly defined terms and conditions.

Another example is voluntary or involuntary termination benefits or limitations. Some contracts attempt to prohibit you from working in the same industry for a year or more. Other contracts limit solicitation of *any* clients. Be careful not to sign any agreement that will make you unemployable for a year or more.

Do not assume you know what the clauses mean. In Georgia, contract language that binds you in some states will not bind you in Georgia, but unless you know Georgia law you may assume you cannot work when you really can.

You need to ensure you have a complete picture of what you are signing before you sign. Just as when you are investing in real estate or stocks, the most money is made when you buy. This is when you have the most leverage. Be sure you use that leverage wisely.

Assume that the worst possible event will happen. The company could become bankrupt. Senior executives could be crooks, liars, and want to harm you. That "trusted" hiring manager could be hit by a Mack truck tomorrow leaving a new boss over you who could be out to eliminate you. A senior management change could result in you being asked to leave, regardless of performance. Possibilities are endless. Be sure you are protected.

Hope for the best. Do not make these negotiations painful to everyone. Reasonable requests made in a reasonable manner are frequently accepted. Be sure to ask—with a smile! Be sure you have professional help even if they are not visible to the hiring company.

Negotiating Terms, Even Without a Contract

Some companies do not offer employment agreements – to anyone. That could be a good thing. That means many of the onerous termination clauses will also be omitted. When the offer is dated, has compensation terms (consideration), and you accept it, you have a contract. The good news is that most state laws will interpret the silence in your favor with common law interpretation. The bad news is that golden handcuffs and exotic options terms will also likely be missing.

I still recommend you obtain legal advice before you sign. There could be another sentence or two with benefits or terms that they may accept and you might love.

Jobs Are Temporary–Your Obligations Are Not

By now many readers may decide to skip the recommendations given. I strongly suggest you reconsider. I have worked with lawyers for over twenty years. I know a lot about the law. I negotiate contracts routinely. However, when your personal security and work life is at risk, you need experts who are current in local state law to be on your side.

The average job today lasts two to three years. There will usually be a lack of income during transitions to the next job, but your financial obligations will continue. You owe it to yourself and to your family to treat this area as seriously as you would a multimillion-dollar contract. Your superiors view their contracts that way and expect that a true professional worth his salt would too. Aren't you that professional?

Chapter Thirteen

Step Twelve: Landed! What Next?

First, congratulations! Second, take a deep breath and continue your new lifelong branding process.

The First Twelve Weeks

I do not need to tell you that the next twelve weeks usually feel like you are drowning in overload. Too much to do and too many long days is to be expected. You need to be contributing as soon as possible. You need to earn the trust and respect of your new associates and get established.

However, do not forget that most jobs today only last two to three years. You are no longer a long-term employee. You are an employee "contract worker."

So what is your game plan?

First, as soon as you accept the position, be sure you notify your network and thank everyone for their help, letting them know that you will "disappear" for a while.

Second, plan to re-emerge after the first twelve weeks to continue your new lifelong business of preparing for your next "contract" (job). Two years will pass quickly. Heaven forbid that the United States is in an economic downturn and you have not kept up your network.

Continuing Your Brand Awareness Campaign

So how do you keep up your network without sending the wrong signals to your current employer? Simple: You are your personal brand. Keep expanding exposure to your brand by attending appropriate events that keep you "plugged in" to maintain relationships you developed earlier and to develop new relationships with those who can help you in the future. These events expect you to discuss your brand. Be sure you continue practicing and improving your message.

Identify yourself with your brand, not the company you currently work for. The company you work for will change. Your brand usually does not change. Feel free to mention who you work for but follow it with what you do (brand), not what your title is for the moment.

One key concept to consider is, "Who are you networking with?" When you land, the tendency is to stop going to networking meetings and to "network" within your church, children's sporting events, non-profit activities, or family activities. Actually, these are good places to let them know your brand. You will want to attend these activities for personal reasons, and you can also develop relationships for future business opportunities.

My recommendation is to be sure you get to know these people on a personal basis and not try to push yourself on them. Ask them about themselves. Ask them what they do for a living. See if you can help them.

Helping Others

No one likes a hard sale. No one likes to be pressured into helping someone. So don't go there – ever. You will only harm your brand.

However, we all need help at some point in time. Only the arrogant believe otherwise. Why not get to know your networks as friends and listen for opportunities to help them? The concept is called "pay it forward." Have you noticed how I keep repeating this phrase?

The concept is that you are thankful for those who helped you in the past. If you feel that no one has ever helped you, then you have a bigger issue to address – lack of appreciation and thankfulness. However, if you realize that mentors and introductions have played a role in your success, then why not "pay it back" to someone else?

Look for opportunities to help others. Do they need an introduction, a referral, help on their brand, marketing document, or resume? When you work a room, don't do it for your own selfish purpose. Look for people to get to know and to see if you can help them. They will usually want to know about you (brand) and how they can help you.

Do this as a lifestyle and you will be amazed how many people will remember you as a class act and someone they can trust to refer to their friends. You will be surprised how others will often expand your network for you.

Besides, it feels good to do the right thing and to help others.

Preparing for Your Next Opportunity

Take another look at the sections on your value proposition and stories. Remember that you had to document the unique values that set you apart from others? Remember that you had to create stories of accomplishments that supported your passion, vision, brand, and value?

Guess what? You will need to continue adding current values and stories built upon the experiences you are getting at your new job today.

First, make a chart of your objectives and how they tie into your story. Then be sure to measure the results. Finally, write down a brief story as you experience it.

Notice that you should be doing this anyway for your annual performance review and for internal communications of your value. This will make you more valuable within the company, help communicate why you should get that promotion and salary increase, and let you be ready for a running start when you get serious about looking for the next saddle to jump on.

These secrets are used by every successful executive. Be sure you are one of them!

Chapter Fourteen

Concluding Remarks

The ROI of Networking

I assume everyone reading this book understands ROI (Return on Investment). You may not have thought about the work of looking for a job as an investment. You may be surprised to learn that the *Whacked Again!* ROI may have a longer- term benefit than your personal financial portfolio! Let's ask a few questions.

- How long does a traditional transition last between jobs? (Industry suggestion is one month for every $10,000 in annual income)
- What if you could reduce that time by 50%? How much money would that mean to you?
- How much money do you expect to make in your new job?
- What if you could come across as a true value-added executive rather than a commodity executive? How much money would that mean to you – each year?
- If your answers were positive to the previous questions, could these impacts help increase your compensation level for the rest of your career?

- If so, how many years are left in your career? How much will the total annuity be worth over the rest of your career?

Now estimate how much going through this process and taking the time will cost you. Divide your total benefit over your future career by this cost. That is my estimate of your ROI.

It is important that you go through this calculation. Why? We often do not "feel" like getting up to network or "feel" like going through the process recommended in this book.

Most of my friends are shocked at the results. I hope you are pleasantly surprised too.

Notice that I did not include increased retirement benefits, increased stock options, or similar incremental but hard to define "uppers."

Is the ROI of this process worth it to you?

Retirement or Passion?

The American way is to plan for retirement and then die. I have heard that most men die within five years of retirement. I guess that means you should never retire! If you saved and invested your money and have been dreaming of hitting the golf fairways, I do not wish to discourage you. Go ahead.

However, many retired executives find themselves bored to death and want to get back to work. Often the spouse becomes tired of the retiree being at home so much and wants to push him out of the house. Maybe that is why the British have so many men's clubs, so they can maintain their dignity while not driving their wives crazy!

Even if you decide to retire, I recommend you consider whether your passion can be continued after retirement. Can you get back into the saddle while still getting retirement pay? Can you start your own company or consult? Perhaps you could read the book *Half Time* and work for a non-profit. If you are really passionate and good at something, you will want to stay active as long as possible. It may actually help you live longer and keep you thrilled at the chase of life to continue building your vision.

If the golf course or other leisure activity is your passion and you can afford it, by all means enjoy it. Perhaps you can squeeze in a few other pursuits such as board memberships, advisory memberships, or even helping in your local community. Everybody would win.

Becoming a Key Resource for Others

No matter where you are in your journey (working hard, changing saddles, or retired) one of the great joys in life is to help others. Others win from your sincere mentoring, referring, or listening.

It is not unusual for other board members, football coaches, soccer parents, church committee members, and non-profit groups to be full of decision makers, influencers, friends of decision makers, and just good people. You might be amazed who you could be standing beside. Many of them can help you.

If you learn your passion, vision, brand, value proposition, and stories, you should be able to communicate to a child or a CEO.

Then you can help others and help others help you. Everybody wins.

Want to Learn More? Join our community at www.WhackedAgain.com.

CPSIA information can be obtained at www.ICGtesting.com
Printed in the USA
239508LV00001B/563/P